TWICE AS GOOD

Practical Tools
To Double
The Impact Of
Your Philanthropy

Joey Savoie

Books
Of
Change

Twice As Good
Practical Tools to Double the Impact of Your Philanthropy

Published by Books Of Change, San Francisco
ISBN: 978-1-968679-04-0 (hardcover),
978-1-968679-05-7 (paperback),
978-1-968679-06-4 (ebook)
LCSH: Career development. Vocational guidance. Altruism. Charities—
Decision making. Social responsibility of business.
HN49.P6 S28 2026
Book layout by Katherine Getta
Author photo by Judith Rensing
Cover design by Trevor Messersmith

Table of Contents

Saving a Life Every Day

The Moment that Changes Everything

> Yuko tasted it first, a slight bitterness on her tongue. The taste came a moment before the smoke stung her eyes and filled her lungs. As she turned the corner, the source revealed itself: an old wooden house. Orange flames flickered through the windows, and inky smoke billowed from cracks in the walls. Hearing a child's scream from inside, Yuko didn't hesitate. No one else was around. She knew she had to help.

Few people have saved someone's life. Those who have say it's a profound and surreal experience. They realize that seeing someone do simple things like walking, laughing, or eating takes on a whole new meaning because they might never have done so again. And the impact doesn't stop there. From family and friends to coworkers and passing acquaintances, dozens of lives are affected. Still, most people might only get one chance in their lifetime to save someone, and running into a burning building comes with great personal risk.

But what if you could save a life every day? It's a rare feat, achieved by the most innovative scientists, the most famous political activists, the most successful NGO founders, and the wisest foundations.

Funders have a unique ability to spark movements and reshape entire fields. Those who prioritize impact, make thoughtful decisions, and use their time strategically can save a life, or multiple lives, for every day they operate. Helping that many people is usually the stuff of superhero movies, yet by combining one's giving with hard work and a little luck, it's possible.

This level of impact is the best reason to start a foundation or engage in grant-making. Throughout history, funders have transformed countless lives and tackled critical problems that might otherwise have been ignored.

This handbook is about how to become such a funder.

Should Grantmakers Follow Their Heart or Their Head?

Most foundations do incredible work and create significant impact, but many also leave considerable potential unrealized. I believe that by applying six straightforward principles (which we call POWERS, an acronym outlined below), you can double the impact of your grants. That's a big win, even for foundations already making a big difference.

When a foundation combines solid research with clear guiding principles, it can amplify its impact, often achieving twice as much as other funders of the same size. Beyond the numbers, this level of impact also brings a deep sense of purpose and meaning to grantmaking.

Unlike many books on philanthropy, this one covers relatively little about the logistics of giving or the case for giving. It instead focuses on principles that directly apply to real-world situations your foundation will encounter, which, when solved well, will increase your impact. Throughout, I will be referring to some standout examples in the real world of philanthropy. I'll also include stories of other foundations (some anonymized for privacy, others slightly fictionalized) to illustrate key lessons and common themes. And when I share cautionary tales or negative examples, they'll usually be composites: not aimed at or based on any one grantmaker, but put together to illustrate a bigger pattern.

The Treehugger vs. the Stockbroker

I should have known the brunch party would spark interesting but challenging conversations. It was always a bit of a risk to mix friends from such different circles. But as I nervously arranged place settings on Sunday morning, I never anticipated being caught between two worldviews quite so dramatically.

To my left sat Lake, her flowing emerald dress and crystal necklace as distinctive as her name. To my right was Ryan, who had arrived in a crisp charcoal suit despite the casual brunch setting, already checking stock information on his phone. I found myself physically and metaphorically in the middle, attempting to bridge two very different approaches to life.

After we narrowly avoided the "Is capitalism fundamentally good or evil?" debate that can derail an entire brunch, the conversation thankfully turned to charitable giving, my favorite topic.

"How do you each think about supporting nonprofits?" I asked, hoping to find common ground.

Lake leaned forward. "You have to follow your heart. The causes that move you emotionally are the ones where you'll make the biggest difference because you'll truly care about the outcomes."

Ryan raised an eyebrow. "If I invested based on emotional attachment, I'd be bankrupt within a week without ever actually making a difference," he replied. "The market rewards disciplined analysis, not feelings."

"So how do you approach charitable giving?" I asked Ryan, trying to keep the conversation constructive.

"Honestly, I rarely do," he admitted. "Markets efficiently solve most problems. People purchase what they need, which drives innovation and improvement."

Lake set down her fork. "What about those with no purchasing power? A person living on a dollar a day, or an endangered species, can't simply 'buy' their way out of suffering."

"Fair point," Ryan conceded. "There might be areas where charities make sense, but most nonprofits I've encountered operate with shocking inefficiency." His eyes lit up as he began describing wasteful practices he'd observed in various organizations.

"That doesn't mean we should stop trying," Lake countered. "I personally know nonprofit founders who work tirelessly because they genuinely care about making a difference."

"I think you're both making valid points," I interjected. "Some nonprofits are indeed ineffective, while others create tremendous value. The real challenge is identifying which is which. How would each of you determine whether a nonprofit is worth supporting?"

"Cold, hard data and analytics," Ryan said definitively.

"A passionate team with a deep understanding of the problem," Lake answered at the same time.

As they continued debating, I realized something important. The nonprofit sector, while small compared to the global economy, contains organizations across the effectiveness spectrum. Lake's compassion ensured she would always support causes that needed help; she never missed a fundraising email from our friend group. Meanwhile, Ryan's analytical mind could spot financial inefficiencies with ease.

I wished I could somehow merge the two of them. Imagine a grantmaker with Lake's genuine compassion and motivation combined with Ryan's rigorous analysis and skepticism. That combination—a heart that cares deeply paired with a head that thinks critically—is precisely what distinguishes the most effective philanthropists I've known.

The most impactful grantmaking happens at the intersection of compassion and analysis. A heart-only approach leads to well-intentioned but potentially ineffective giving, while a head-only approach might optimize for efficiency but fall far short of one's giving potential. The best philanthropists cultivate both: they're driven by authentic compassion to make a difference and cultivate a legacy to be proud of, but they also apply rigorous analysis to ensure their resources create the greatest possible impact.

If you've picked up this book, you likely already have the heart part covered. Your commitment to philanthropy shows a genuine desire to improve lives and tackle important challenges. That compassion is the foundation of meaningful grantmaking.

Throughout this book, we'll explore how pairing that compassion with solid tools and frameworks can amplify your impact without diminishing your passion. Think of it as adding new instruments to your philanthropic orchestra rather than replacing any that are already playing. When heart and head work in harmony, the music of your giving can reach more people and resonate more deeply than either could accomplish alone.

What Is the Point of This Book?

Remember that irritating kid in class who would always ask the teacher, "*What's the point of this lesson?*" I was that kid. It's a question that many of us feel, somewhere between a passing curiosity and an insatiable need to know, and it's a question every non-fiction book should answer.

One question has stuck with me for as long as I can remember: how can we do the most good? After working with around a dozen NGOs, founding three of my own, and building Charity Entrepreneurship (a program that's launched over 50 new organizations and been called "the Hogwarts of do-gooding"), I moved to the grantmaker side, where I made a lot of funding decisions. Eventually, I set up a training program that has trained and supported dozens of foundations. I finally feel I have something concretely useful to add to the question of how to do the most good and have the most impact, and this book aims to distill knowledge from both sides of the grantmaking ecosystem.

Why read this book instead of any other? You could be rock climbing right now! There are two key reasons. First, through a series of concrete, easy-to-implement examples, this book answers one key question: How can you do the most good as a grantmaker? Along the way, it also answers several related questions you might have about becoming a successful grantmaker.

Second, this book is written for a specific type of person.

Who Is This Book for?

We already know the short answer: people who care about answering the question of how to do the most good. But that answer includes virtually everyone.

So here's a better answer. This book is for funders and grantmakers who:

1. Are considering making major changes or improvements in their grantmaking, or are just setting up their giving, and

2. Care deeply about increasing the impact of their giving, even if that means making fewer spontaneous or prestigious grants.

Fundamentally, this book is built for those who want to double the impact of their grantmaking and are excited to put in the time and consideration it takes to make that happen. My aim is to be helpful, content-dense, and entertaining, in that order. Ultimately, I firmly believe that with just a short book, it's possible to double your impact.

What Are the Big Questions That Matter to Grantmakers?

Over the last decade, I've worked with dozens of foundations. Despite their wide range of topics, sizes, and personalities, many share the same core questions:

1. What is the best area for me to focus on?

2. How do I make sure I am not a bad grantmaker?

3. How do I get better at grantmaking?

4. What is normal or best practice in the grantmaking field?

5. How can I communicate with others—family, friends, philanthropic communities—about grantmaking?

This book aims to help answer these questions in an interesting, practical way, with as little unnecessary fluff as possible. Each chapter and paragraph is designed to help busy grantmakers navigate these challenges more effectively.

How Is the Book Organized?

Scope

We begin with the first question: *What is the best area for me to focus on?* While there's no single correct answer, we offer plenty of guidance on how to define a scope that's the right size, neglected, and narrow enough that you cover 2–20% of your chosen field, plus a fun flowchart to help you identify areas worth exploring.

In this chapter, we will go deeper into three key ways to narrow your focus:

• Cause area

• Geographic scope

• NGO size

POWERS

The bulk of the book helps you to become the best grantmaker in your chosen focus area(s), distilling the most useful lessons into six core "powers" of good grantmaking. As you might have guessed, POWERS is an acronym to help you remember them.

Can just six principles make you a perfect grantmaker? Probably not, but they can get you 90% of the way there and double your impact even for those with limited time or logistical constraints. And for those who want to dive deeper, we've included extensive appendices.

Here are the six powers of good grantmaking:

• **P**rice tag: You should know the price tag and how much impact it buys for every grant you give.

- **O**ptions: Compare 10 or more options for every grant you give.

- **W**ho: Decide who should research and decide on your grants.

- **E**valuate: Set a concrete NGO benchmark, the best option that could handle 100% of your funding.

- **R**educe: Reduce the time you take from NGOs; aim for a maximum of 2 hours + 1 additional hour per $50k of grant.

- **S**ubstance: Focus on substance over style and know how the charity works.

Building your community

The final section explores how to build your grantmaking community, whether through conversations with family, co-granting partnerships, or joining structured networks. We break this down into two core approaches:

- Amplifying: *If you want to go fast, go alone; if you want to go far, go together. Your network is typically ten times more powerful than you are as an individual.*

- Connecting: *You are the sum of your five closest peers. Surround yourself with great grantmakers, and you'll make better grants.*

Conclusion

The book wraps up with two real-world stories of outstanding grantmakers: one large and one small but mighty. There is also an appendix that goes into more detail on some of the key concepts introduced in the book and a list of resources for those who want to learn more.

CHAPTER 1

Scope

Pick a scope that is neglected and narrow enough that you are 2–20% of the field.

Why Donating to What Is on the News Is Old News

When the earthquake hit, Izzy's NGO was perfectly placed to help. It ran health clinics across one of the most devastated cities in a low-income country, where medicine, even at the best of times, was often unavailable. The earthquake made everything harder: broken roads hindered deliveries, crumbling clinics were unsafe to work in, and injured staff couldn't come to work. But Izzy faced a more immediate and unexpected problem: she couldn't keep up with the influx of donations. The checks kept coming in, turning what should have been an NGO's dream into a nightmare.

Since the earthquake, there has been an outpouring of support for the affected countries. Izzy's previously unknown NGO was highlighted by a major international newspaper, suddenly putting it in front of millions. Among those millions were funders and influencers, whose attention amplified the impact, leading to a huge increase in donations. Too many donations was a problem Izzy never thought she'd face. But now it truly was. Money wasn't the only thing needed to run an NGO. It also needed staff to take action, partners to implement programs, and medical goods to buy.

Izzy's NGO couldn't possibly spend money as effectively as it had when times were lean, especially with the pressure to spend ten times last year's budget in just a few months. Izzy ended up doing what most NGOs do when they get flooded: some of the money got locked away in savings accounts, but a lot went towards costs they'd usually be more cautious about. She bought an overpriced medical device that was shipped to a hospital without the electricity to power it, gave a decent bump in pay to herself and her staff, and signed a big contract with a partner who ended up doing a poor job. When money was so abundant and time so short, mistakes like this were cheap and easy.

Izzy often thought that if just 10% of those donors had given before the earthquake, she could have done much more good. She wasn't alone: most of the NGOs in the city were thinking the exact same thing.

A common way for someone to hear about a new NGO or impact area is through a newspaper, talk show, or podcast. However, there's a strange phenomenon: simply by being seen by many people, a cause not only becomes less neglected but can even become overfunded. Izzy's NGO might have been a great impact investment the year before the earthquake, but donating to it after it had already been widely publicized was a much weaker investment. Few NGOs can handle tripling of their budgets in under a year, and many of the most cost-effective actions are preventative, not reactive. The best value NGOs are often those that are less well-known.

Scope is about identifying the area to focus on and defining the boundaries of what you want to work on. One of the core principles of scope is identifying areas others might overlook, whether they are other grantmakers, individual donors, or governments. The best opportunities are often those no one else is funding, even though they should be. Finding these areas takes a bit of extra digging. A decent rule of thumb: if it's one of the top five most popular topics at a party, it's probably not a neglected philanthropic opportunity.

Of course, knowing what to avoid doesn't solve the question of how to discover new and promising NGOs, and how to focus on the best opportunities instead of whatever is currently trending.

Interactions of Scope

When narrowing the focus of a foundation, three primary factors come into play: **cause area, geography**, and **NGO size**. These factors interact with one another. If you end up with a broad cause area, you'll need to narrow it down further by considering NGO size and geographic focus. Conversely, a broad geographic focus will require a more specific cause area to keep your pool of options manageable. The key is to adjust these three levers in combination until you land on a scope that's right for the size of your foundation.

Measure twice, cut once: narrowing in a smart way

Most foundations narrow too little or too early. Narrowing is essential, but doing it wisely is what separates a poorly scoped foundation from one with a clear specialization.

Narrowing too early: Many foundations choose their NGO size, geographic focus, and cause area relatively early, often without deep research. In some ways, it may feel easier not to narrow down significantly. Conducting initial research and refining your focus is one of the clearest ways to increase your philanthropic impact, and it will save a lot of time in the long run. In other words, carefully select your instrument before purchasing it, then become a master at playing it.

Narrowing too little: Trying to address every issue is as futile as trying to play every instrument in an orchestra. Specialization is necessary to excel and become a key contributor to a larger philanthropic movement. We need to narrow down to areas where we can identify the top NGOs. An open book of possibilities may seem exciting, but it can also become overwhelming and make comparisons extremely difficult. In practice, good NGOs often avoid applying to foundations where the fit is unclear.

If I had to distill this entire section down to a single sentence, it would be: "Pick a scope neglected and narrow enough that you are 2–20% of the field." This concrete range forces a level of focus that allows you to become a great grantmaker, and gives a sense of what might make an area too small or too large. Seeking out neglected areas and refining the focus until the size is right can lead to a significant increase in impact.

Moral circles

Back when we were living in caves, the number of people a given human cared about was very small: just the members of their immediate family. Over time, humans had to collaborate with more and more people and engage in complex social interactions, gradually developing empathy and concern for a broader group. Families became tribes, tribes became villages. At one point in time, only white landholding men could vote, but over time, voting rights were expanded to include other genders, races, and socioeconomic groups.

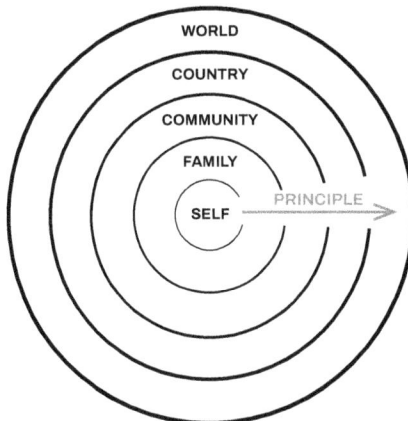

Over thousands of years, this empathy has extended even further to encompass entire nations and global concerns. Now, it's not unusual for someone to care deeply about victims of a natural disaster on the other side of the world, or about an animal they've only ever seen in movies. These would have been unimaginable feats for our ancestors.

This trend is sometimes called the *expanding moral circle*, the idea that our circles of care have widened over time to include more beings. It's tempting to think we've reached the end of the process and that our circle now includes everyone it should. But many beings still remain, for all practical purposes, outside most people's moral circles.

But how does this connect to grantmaking?

It directly connects to your scope. In general, the more people tend to think about moral circles, the broader those circles become. This can happen through deliberate thought (people who study ethical philosophy often extend moral concern to animals) or through experience, such as travel, which can increase global empathy. Our moral circles have expanded, but there are still limits to how many beings we can include in these circles. In other words, our circle has an edge.

There's no definitive answer to who should be in your moral circle or how much weight each group should be given. But it's helpful to find the edge of your circle for two reasons:

1. **You may expand your circle over time.** When I first started learning about animal issues, I could accept that mammals like dogs, cats, cows, and pigs deserved moral concern, but I was skeptical when it came to birds. After learning more about chickens (how they react to pain, their brain structures, how they learn), I became convinced they mattered, too. The same thing happened later with my beliefs about fish.

2. **The edge is often where you can do the most good.** The beings or causes you're just starting to care about, whether fish, faraway humans, or less "cute" animals, tend to be the ones most neglected by others, too. And often, it's where the fewest people are paying attention that your grant can have the biggest impact.

Next, we'll discuss in detail how you can maximize the impact of your giving by focusing on the three aspects of scope: cause area, geographic area, and NGO size.

Choosing a Cause Area

The most important way to narrow

Almost every grantmaker and foundation has some sort of cause area focus. Given that there are hundreds of small cause areas and dozens of broad ones, we've prepared a few questions that can help you narrow your cause area. At the end of this chapter, there's a flowchart with questions to help sort you into one of 12 cause areas. These 12 categories roughly reflect the major areas of philanthropic spending, either among impact-focused donors or across the broader private giving sector. (We haven't included religious giving, as people rarely change their views on that based on a book like this).

Before we get to the chart, we'll walk through some of the considerations of the key choices you'll face.

How big a factor is evidence that the project works?

The first question that can help us decide which cause area to focus on is how important evidence is. Some areas are well studied, with dozens of randomized controlled trials (some of the strongest forms of evidence available). Examples include many global health interventions, such as malaria prevention and vaccinations. Others have relatively little data—maybe just a few case studies or charity-produced research, rather than neutral evaluations by external actors. Examples include education for economic growth, air pollution reduction, and wild animal welfare. Yet others are in the middle, such as tuberculosis control or plant-based and alt-protein advocacy as drivers of sustainability and animal welfare. But there are strong arguments for supporting cause areas on both ends of the evidence spectrum.

The case for evidence being a major factor in picking a cause: three arguments in favor

1) Most things don't work, and what works is often surprising

Sometimes a trend catches fire in the charity world. That was the case with DARE (Drug Abuse Resistance Education), a program so popular it ran in 75% of U.S. schools at its peak in the 1980s and '90s. But multiple studies found that DARE didn't reduce drug use. Some studies even found an *increase* in substance abuse caused by DARE. Sadly, there are numerous examples of NGO programs that backfire and achieve the opposite of their intended goals, too: food aid programs that ultimately increase food scarcity, or anti-crime programs that lead to higher crime rates.

More common than backfiring are interventions that simply don't work at all. Few charities set out to fail, and few donors are eager to fund studies that might reveal failure. Yet many well-studied NGOs and charitable interventions yield disappointing results. The world is too complex to assume we know what works without proper evidence, and even small changes in location or delivery can make the difference between success and failure. If it's hard to predict what works in the NGO world (and many things don't) then having a high bar for evidence is the best way forward.

2) Science has a great track record

The scientific method has delivered enormous progress, from medicine to engineering to agriculture. Compared to other ways of finding truth (e.g., intuition, tradition, authority), science has outperformed. This is especially important when it comes to complex NGO interventions, where there are many chances for efforts to go wrong. Historically, foundations that rely on science and evidence (the Gates Foundation, for example) have achieved outsized impact.

3) It's how the rest of the world works

When a new drug is developed, it undergoes multiple trials to determine its effectiveness and how it compares to existing alternatives. The same goes for most consumer products: we require evidence for safety and efficacy. NGOs tackle some of the most important problems of our time and should be held to similar standards of rigor.

To help you get a sense of whether this strategy may be right for you, here are some traits commonly found in grantmakers who prioritize a high-evidence approach:

- They tend to be more skeptical or questioning than other funders.

- They often come from evidence-based fields like medicine, the hard sciences, or statistics.

- They typically dive deep into topics and focus more on depth than breadth, spending more time on each decision than their peers.

- They're more likely to have spent time in the field and seen firsthand how difficult it can be to execute a plan once it meets reality.

- They tend to be more concerned about downside risks, such as causing harm or failing to have any impact at all.

The case for evidence being a minor factor in picking a cause: three good arguments

1) It allows you to pick areas that score higher on other factors

One of the clearest reasons not to prioritize evidence too highly is that it often requires a fairly direct tradeoff with other important considerations. For example, many grantmakers place a high value on cost-effectiveness, measuring or estimating how many years of education or health a charity can deliver per dollar spent. That makes sense: we want our money to do as much good as possible, and cost is a big driver of that. However, when optimizing for both evidence and cost-effectiveness, you often end up compromising on both.

2) Some areas lack evidence for valid reasons (size, measurability)

Some philanthropic areas lend themselves to high-quality studies, while others don't. For instance, long-shot policy work (e.g., raising taxes on tobacco) might be highly impactful but challenging to study rigorously. Other areas may be so small that a $1 million study would consume a significant portion of the total funding (e.g., if only $3 million per year is spent on mental health in a country). There have been meaningful philanthropic wins in areas where strong evidence was previously difficult to obtain. The Green Revolution, a period of crop innovation that saved millions of lives, began in a highly speculative Research and Development (R&D) space. In some areas, it may be worth taking a shot, even if many attempts don't pan out.

3) Private philanthropy can take more risks

Government grantmaking is often constrained by bureaucracy, political incentives, and long timelines. It tends to be risk-averse, favoring predictable, well-studied programs. Private philanthropy, on the other hand, has more flexibility. It can fill gaps where governments are unable or unwilling to act, especially in high-risk, low-evidence spaces. If the funder is open to uncertainty, private money can fund what others can't. That makes lower-evidence opportunities potentially more appealing for private grantmakers than for public institutions.

The following traits are more commonly found in grantmakers who downplay evidence:

- They tend to work more on systems change or political topics.
- They often come from fields where evidence is harder to obtain (e.g., philosophy, academia, political science).

- They tend to be faster-moving and more opportunistic.

- They're often more optimistic, open-minded, novelty-focused, and risk-seeking.

The case for evidence being a middling factor in picking a cause: three good arguments

1) Diminishing returns on evidence

A strong case for giving evidence some weight without letting it dominate is that evidence becomes less valuable the more you have of it. If you're working in an area with zero studies, going from 0 to 1 makes a huge difference. But few donors would get excited about funding a study that takes an area from 15 to 16 studies. This suggests it may be better to think about evidence in terms of passing a threshold and looking for areas with "good enough" evidence that aren't yet over-studied. A cause with a study or two under its belt expands your options while still filtering out areas that are totally unstudied or already shown not to work.

2) Possibility for evidence creation

Giving some weight to evidence also opens the door to working in areas where evidence could be created. Mental health is a good example: while it hasn't been investigated as much as physical health, it's not inherently hard to study. A grantmaker could help build a significantly better evidence base. This only makes sense, though, if generating new evidence could change your (or others') decisions. It may also rule out highly polarized topics, like gun control in the U.S., where even strong new data might not shift many minds.

3) Generalization of evidence as an alternative

Sometimes you can't find direct evidence for the cause or intervention you're interested in, but you can find it nearby. Movements and sectors often borrow lessons from each other. If you can apply what worked in one space to another, you may get many of the benefits of evidence without the cost. For example, the smaller animal movement might borrow evidence on tactics that have worked for the climate movement, or alcohol taxation might use evidence from the far more established field of tobacco taxation. Generalizability is tricky, as things often generalize less than we expect, but it still beats having no evidence at all.

You see the following traits more commonly in grantmakers who follow a middle-evidence strategy:

- They tend to work with younger charities or in areas that have some established metrics but also some risk.

- They often come from backgrounds like management, entrepreneurship, consulting, or social sciences—fields where evidence is used, but full meta-analyses are rare.

- They tend to fall in the middle of many debates or have more moderate personalities.

Evidence as a choice

Overall, your stance on evidence can dramatically change which cause areas you think are best to focus on, and it tends to be a question you'll face both when comparing cause areas and comparing charities in the same area. It is one of the most significant ways to help narrow down which cause area might be a good fit for you. But it's only one of the top three questions. Next is a question based more on your morals and ethics.

Who matters ethically? Would you rather help 1,000 animals or one human?

Thinking back to when we discussed moral circles, one of the big related considerations is whether or not to include animals in your moral circle, and if you do, how much to weigh them. Here are three reasons why you might include them:

1) Consistency: We already care about some animals

Anyone who has had a family pet has typically already experienced deep empathy for an animal. Dogs and cats are often seen and treated like members of the family, with people spending on them and shaping their lifestyle (such as choosing a home close to a park) with their needs in mind. If we care for these animals, it implies that animals are worthy of moral concern and that charitable projects focusing on animals could be worth investing in. Day-to-day donations also bear this out, with people donating to both homeless shelters and dog shelters in similar ways. It's hard to draw a clear line between dogs, pigs, and elephants on most moral scales. Exactly which animals matter, and how much, is a complex question, but the idea that at least some animals matter significantly is consistent with how most people act in everyday life.

2) It seems like animals can suffer—and if so, they suffer a lot

"The question is not, Can they reason?, nor Can they talk? But can they suffer?"
—Jeremy Bentham

Few people would stand by and let their dog be hurt. Indeed, there are signs that dogs can even have nightmares, experience PTSD, and maintain complex social relationships. But the research becomes more surprising when we look at animals we don't commonly associate with these behaviors. It's not just mammals: birds, fish, and invertebrates all show some surprising evidence that they can experience and try to avoid pain. Of course, we can't know for sure what the experience is like, but it's not unreasonable to make some generalizations. If you lost an arm, it would hurt, and most animals, from birds to bumblebees, show similar avoidance of pain. Their responses even change in similar ways to ours when painkillers are administered.

Our treatment of animals leaves a lot to be desired. While dogs and cats in high-income countries are often protected by robust animal welfare laws, most animals are not. In many cases, especially in factory farming, they are treated as objects, with little to no regard for their pain or suffering. Some of the worst suffering in the world today likely occurs on factory farms. For those unfamiliar, the scale and severity can be shocking: imagine if a dog lived in a kennel the bulk of her life, had her tail and ears cut off at birth without painkillers, and only lived two years before being turned into a meal, and you get close to what many animals go through. The scale is also frightening, with there being about five of these animals around for every single human.

3) It's really neglected and cheap to help animals, so it might be worth it even with a huge discount

Caring about animals is one thing, but how much does one have to care for the issue to be worth considering animals as a target area for charitable donations? It turns out the numbers are pretty stark. Animals have no vote and no purchasing power, so even the easiest goals for welfare are often unmet despite trivial costs. Just like humans, some animals are more neglected than others depending on species and location (for example, a dog in a high-income country is in a far better position than a pig in the same country, or a street dog in a low-income one).

Although this is a sad reality, it creates an exciting opportunity for philanthropists. Often, it's cheaper and easier to help thousands of animals than a single person. Our best guess is that it could cost around $3,000 to save a human life, and under a dollar to spare a hen from life in a cramped cage, where crowding and stress often lead to chronic suffering. Given that philanthropy can't support every area, and private philanthropy aims to support those that society would otherwise overlook, animal welfare seems like a promising area to consider.

The case against moral concern for animals

1) Caring doesn't mean being willing to make tradeoffs

Moral tradeoffs are hard. Although, as a philanthropist, there is no avoiding the need to prioritize some areas over others (and thus implicitly trade off between different moral outcomes and lives), some tradeoffs might be too extreme. There is still significant human suffering in the world, and a philanthropist might take the stance that humans should always be the first priority, regardless of the numbers or severity of suffering experienced.

2) The science of suffering is still uncertain in many areas

Although more research emerges every day, definitively proving that animals suffer is still tricky, and by some standards, impossible. Some philosophers are even skeptical that other *humans* can suffer, and every move away from your own experience towards the edge of your moral circle adds complexity. Animals are fundamentally different in some ways, and because they can't speak, it's hard to know how they comprehend the world. The evidence base for suffering also varies by species. For example, evidence is considerably less developed for fish than for larger animals like cows or dogs. Particularly for risk-averse funders, it may feel challenging to spend significant philanthropic capital on animals you're not sure can even experience pain and suffering. This might lead to focusing only on particular species or solely on humans.

3) Flow-through effects of helping humans

Some might care deeply about animals but still not prioritize them due to the second-order effects of helping humans. A person pulled out of poverty can, in theory, go on to help others, contribute to economic growth, or create a technology that benefits the world. Regardless of your views on animals, it's unlikely a panda will invent the next technological breakthrough. Similarly, it's often easier to rally support for human-focused causes than for animal ones. If much of your impact depends on convincing others who may never support animal charities, it might make sense to deprioritize them as a focus area. This can be especially relevant in family philanthropy, where you need to choose areas of focus that multiple people can agree on.

Do animals make the cut?

The case of whether you include animals or not can be a contentious issue, with people having strong feelings on both sides. Animals are near and dear to many of our hearts, yet it is still rare for a private foundation to focus on them. In any case, your cause selection work is not done, particularly if you do not want to focus exclusively on animals. That's because you still must consider one final question.

What outcomes matter most: wealth, health, or something else?

Out of all the decisions in philanthropy, one of the most important (and the one that will most affect your selected focus areas) is deciding what outcomes you care about most.

Charity comparison becomes considerably easier when you're working within the same outcome framework. For instance, comparing two charities that aim to improve income is far easier than comparing one focused on income and another on health. Below are some of the primary metrics used across outcome frameworks in the charity world, with a summary of their pros and cons, and what you might expect to achieve with $1 million of thoughtful grantmaking in each area.

The case for health

Health is a field with hundreds of challenges, from illness to physical impairment. One thing that makes health an appealing ultimate goal for grantmaking is that the global health community has collectively developed a metric to compare a wide range of conditions: the DALY (disability-adjusted life year). Losing 1 DALY is equivalent to losing a full year of healthy life. A severe impairment, such as a year lived with schizophrenia, is assigned a DALY weight of 0.57, whereas something milder, like lower back pain, might be 0.06. This system enables analytical cross-comparison between different health interventions and charities. DALYs are far from perfect, but they're widely used and well-documented, making them one of the most consistent and useful metrics in cause selection.

Health also has other advantages beyond the DALY framework. It's often rated as extremely important by people when asked what matters most, and it's seen as essential to the quality of life. People living with chronic illness are often willing to trade off heavily on other metrics like income in exchange for being healthy again. Health is also relatively objective and transferable: if a treatment cures tuberculosis in one country, it's likely to cure it in another, in a way that's not always true for interventions in other areas.

DALYs and health more broadly are almost universally valued. They're often a good bar to beat for other metrics. If you're unsure what health outcome to prioritize, starting with DALYs is a solid choice. With $1 million spent on health, you could, for example, save approximately 300 lives or cure a lifetime of blindness for 600 people.

The case for income and wealth

Income is also a fairly well-understood and easy-to-measure metric. It's something we all deal with and have an intuitive sense of. In some ways, it's even clearer than health, as it avoids DALY-style assumptions about how much different ailments matter. Income is also an extremely flexible benefit: if someone gains more income or wealth, they can often spend it to improve any of the other outcomes, such as health or personal happiness. That said, if your goal is to improve a specific metric like health, targeting it directly will often get you more bang for your buck.

Many common philanthropic donations are closely tied to income, livelihoods, and wealth. For example, education or job creation interventions are often measured by their return on investment (ROI) in future income. A donation to this kind of intervention typically creates more than just the cash value of a direct transfer to the recipient. A good but achievable return might be around 1:5, meaning $1 of donation could lead to $5 of additional income over time[1].

Income can be a compelling metric if you have strong trust in markets to solve problems, or if you prefer a more freedom-focused or libertarian approach that supports people in solving their own problems. Income also interacts interestingly with wealth: the more someone has, the less valuable each additional dollar tends to be. This means doubling someone's income from $1,000 to $2,000 is far more impactful than increasing it from $50,000 to $51,000. It's partly due to this dynamic that the highest-return opportunities often come from helping people in extreme poverty.

As indicated above, with $1 million spent on income generation, you can typically create about $5 million in additional income or wealth.

The case for subjective well-being

Subjective well-being is a new metric with a simple idea: we should measure what makes people happier. This is partially inspired by surprising findings on hedonic adaptation, which show that events influence our happiness for a shorter duration and to a lesser degree than we anticipate. For example, both lottery winners and people who lost use of their legs reported close to baseline happiness less than a year later. Subjective well-being, in many ways, is closer to the "real" truth of what we want, but it's far harder to measure, less consistent in its results, and less commonly used.

The most established field that uses subjective well-being is mental health, particularly higher-income mental health. Subjective well-being experts can measure affect on a number of scales, but often the simplest is finding out how happy someone is on a scale from one to 10. The measurement can be used multiple times over the course of someone's life and can thus be used to find the problems that most influence well-being.

With $1 million spent on subjective well-being, you could prevent nine months of severe depression for 4,760 people.[2]

The case for human rights

Human rights is a field focused on protecting fundamental freedoms, from preventing torture to ensuring fair trials to defending the rights of refugees. The sector doesn't have a standardized metric like health or income, though some organizations use Rights Violation Indices (RVIs) to track the severity and frequency of abuses. Impact is often measured through case numbers, people protected, or systemic wins achieved through legal precedent or policy reform.

Unlike health interventions, where outcomes are relatively predictable, human rights work tends to have highly variable returns. A single strategic litigation case might set a precedent that protects thousands of people's rights, while direct service programs offer more predictable help, but often at a higher cost per person. When surveyed, people consistently rank basic rights and freedoms as essential to well-being, often seeing them as a precondition for other quality-of-life factors.

With $1 million spent on human rights, you could fund legal aid for around 285 legal cases, including asylum claims, human trafficking victims, and labor rights violations.[3]

The case for the environment

Environmental interventions tackle a mix of interconnected challenges such as climate change, biodiversity loss, and pollution. The field has developed several useful metrics, including tons of CO_2 equivalent (tCO_2e) calculations for climate impact, species extinction rates for biodiversity, and various pollution indices. Climate change, in particular, has emerged as a well-measured area where cost-effectiveness can be directly compared using carbon pricing and verified reduction and removal projects.

With $1 million spent on environmental NGOs, you can typically remove around 1 million tons of CO_2, or about the carbon footprint of 60,000 people for a year.[4]

The case for the arts

Arts is a field that spans many forms of cultural expression and creativity, from visual and performing arts to community-based cultural programs. While it lacks a unified metric like DALYs, the sector uses tools such as the Cultural Vitality Index (CVI), which tracks things like participation rates, economic contribution, and community engagement. A year of arts education might lead to a range of benefits from better academic outcomes to stronger emotional well-being and social connection.

Arts interventions face greater measurement challenges than health programs, but they tend to show consistent, if modest, positive effects across many areas. When surveyed, people often rank cultural access and creative expression as important for their quality of life, though usually below health or basic needs. Arts programs also create spillover effects in education, mental health, and community cohesion, though results can vary more by context. A successful youth orchestra in one city might not transfer easily to another due to cultural and social factors.

With $1 million spent on the arts, you can typically fund 3,000 student-years of arts education.[5]

The flowchart

Putting it all together, here's a short, incomplete, but useful flowchart that can help guide you toward some cause areas to look into. In the foundation training program, we've guided dozens of grantmakers through this process, achieving about 85% accuracy in connecting them with a cause area that felt right for them. It's helpful, but only as a starting point. It might make sense to read the cause area paragraphs that follow if you're unsure about a decision or if you land in different places when you go through the chart more than once.

CAUSE AREA FLOWCHART

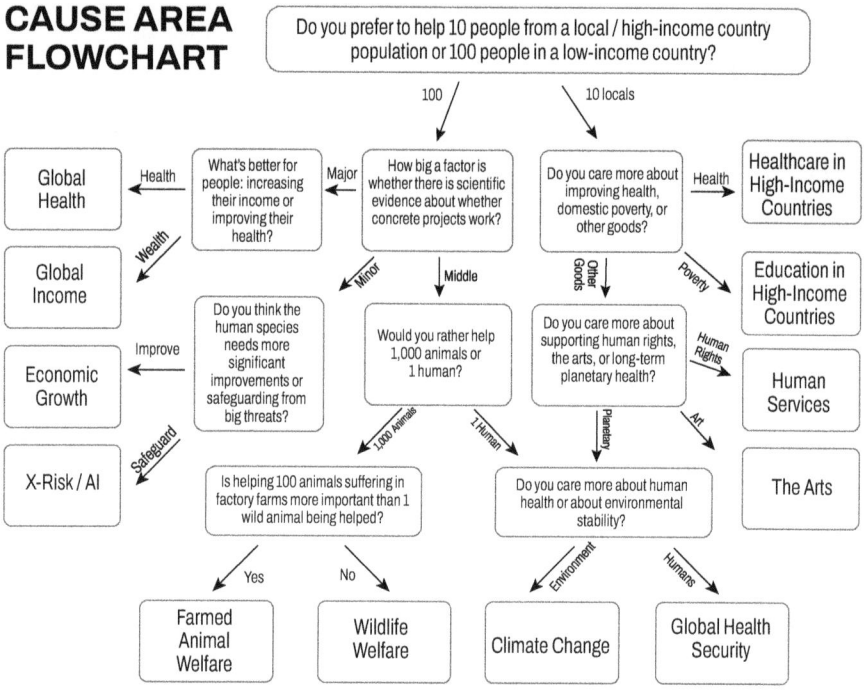

Do you prefer to help 10 people from a local / high-income country population or 100 people in a low-income country?

100 / 10 locals

Global Health ←— Health —— What's better for people: increasing their income or improving their health? ←— Major —— How big a factor is whether there is scientific evidence about whether concrete projects work? ←— 100 — | — 10 locals —→ Do you care more about improving health, domestic poverty, or other goods? —— Health —→ **Healthcare in High-Income Countries**

Global Income ←— Wealth

Minor ↓ | Middle ↓ | Other Goods ↓ | Poverty → **Education in High-Income Countries**

Economic Growth ←— Improve —— Do you think the human species needs more significant improvements or safeguarding from big threats?

Would you rather help 1,000 animals or 1 human?

Do you care more about supporting human rights, the arts, or long-term planetary health? —— Human Rights —→ **Human Services**

X-Risk / AI ←— Safeguard —— Is helping 100 animals suffering in factory farms more important than 1 wild animal being helped?

1,000 Animals ↓ | 1 Human ↓ | Planetary ↓ | Art → **The Arts**

Do you care more about human health or environmental stability?

Yes ↓ No ↓ | Environment ↓ Humans ↓

Farmed Animal Welfare | **Wildlife Welfare** | **Climate Change** | **Global Health Security**

A million-dollar question

Before we dive into descriptions of cause areas, I want to include a more direct comparison. Below is a rough estimate of what you might be able to "buy" in each cause area with a $1 million grant. This kind of direct comparison is rarely made, but ultimately, it's the kind of tradeoff every grantmaker is making when they choose to focus on one area over another.

Cause area	What $1M of grantmaking might buy
Global health	Assuming a median of $5,000 per life saved, save 200 lives by distributing malaria-preventing bed nets in Ghana. [6]
High-income health	Save 40 lives, e.g., by supporting smoking cessation programs.[7] Or run happiness skills courses reaching thousands. [8]
Global income	Create $5 million in wealth, for example, by funding improved school lesson plans in India.[9]
High-income education	Support 40–50 participants through a career training program, generating $7,000–8,000 in annual earnings gains per person in the years that follow.[10]

Economic growth	Generate $100 million in economic growth over 12 years through high-leverage policy research.[11]
Pandemics	Fund a research team to produce influential policy reports and run a tabletop outbreak simulation.[12]
Climate	Remove around 1 million tons of CO_2, for example, by advocating for government support of clean energy innovation.[13]
Farmed animals	Help 3 million animals, for example, by advocating against the most painful methods of confinement (e.g., cages).[14]
Wildlife welfare	Conduct multiple research projects on welfare indicators across species, advancing the field of welfare biology.[15]
Rights and justice	Provide legal support to retry dozens of excessive punishment cases, potentially saving hundreds of years of unjust incarceration.[16]
X-risk/AI	Fund 3–4 technical AI safety research projects or support a 4-person research team for a year.[17]
Arts	Deliver 4,000 student years of arts education.[18]

Main cause areas

Global Health: Global health interventions offer an extraordinary opportunity to save lives at remarkably low cost, around $3,000 per life saved through proven programs like malaria prevention. This cause area stands on firm moral ground across diverse ethical perspectives (no one defends preventable child deaths) and benefits from exceptionally strong evidence, with organizations like Malaria Consortium demonstrating transparent impact through rigorous implementation and monitoring. While attracting significant funding from major players like the Gates Foundation and multilateral organizations, global health remains underfunded compared to healthcare spending in wealthy nations. A $1 million investment can save approximately 300 lives through cost-effective interventions such as bed-net distribution, making this area a **compelling choice for donors seeking proven impact with robust evidence**.

Income and Livelihoods: Income-focused interventions empower people in poverty to build sustainable economic well-being through various approaches from direct cash transfers to education and entrepreneurship development. Programs like One Acre Fund demonstrate remarkable efficiency: $1 million can boost annual income by 40–50% for 5,000 farming families (affecting approximately 25,000 people), while Pratham can improve educational outcomes for around 100,000 children in India with the same investment. Unlike prescriptive aid, many income interventions give recipients decision-making agency, potentially improving nutrition, health, education, and resilience against shocks. **This space is highly promising for those who value autonomy or income over health.**

Policy-Focused Economic Growth: Economic policy reform represents a high-leverage approach to development, where successful advocacy can unlock billions in value by removing systemic barriers like restrictive immigration policies, excessive land-use regulations, or trade barriers. Organizations like Copenhagen Consensus Center demonstrate remarkable return potentials, with each dollar invested potentially influencing $1,000 in more effective government spending. The primary challenges include the scarcity of proven organizations, attribution difficulties in measuring impact, politically charged evidence, and long-time horizons with uncertain outcomes. **For donors comfortable with higher-risk, higher-reward investments and potentially contentious political dynamics, policy reform offers scale potential that is hard for other areas to compete with,** though success requires patience and tolerance for the complexity of navigating ideological divides to achieve meaningful systemic change.

X-risk/AI: AI safety and existential risk reduction aim to ensure that advanced AI remains aligned with human values and controllable, even as it surpasses human capabilities. Organizations like Redwood Research and Epoch work on critical technical alignment problems and strategic forecasting, with $1 million potentially funding three to four technical research projects, or a year's work for a specialized research team developing safety techniques that could influence implementation at major AI labs. The space has attracted significant funding from Coefficient Giving and increasing attention from tech companies like Microsoft, Google DeepMind, and Anthropic; it remains characterized by substantial uncertainty about risk timelines, the nature of threats, and the effectiveness of proposed solutions. The field faces talent constraints and academic credibility challenges, with few established metrics for evaluating progress. **For donors comfortable with higher-risk, potentially higher-reward investments, this area offers a chance to address what could be humanity's most consequential technological transition.**

Farmed Animal Welfare: This is a way to help alleviate the immense suffering of over 80 billion land animals and trillions of aquatic animals raised annually in conditions often comparable to human prisons or worse. Organizations like the Humane League demonstrate remarkable cost-effectiveness, potentially improving conditions for 8–120 million animals per $1 million donated through corporate campaigns that secure higher welfare standards from food companies. Despite this extraordinary scale and impact potential, the cause remains severely neglected, with animal charities receiving less than 1.5% of all donations and farmed animals receiving only a fraction of that, despite representing over 99% of animals used by humans. While the field faces challenges in impact measurement, philosophical disagreement about animal moral worth, and powerful industry opposition, it **offers donors focused on reducing suffering an unparalleled opportunity to affect enormous numbers of sentient beings at a relatively low cost per individual helped, addressing one of the largest sources of preventable suffering today.**

Wildlife Welfare: This effort addresses the well-being of animals in natural environments, potentially benefiting billions to trillions of animals by combining traditional conservation with emerging concerns about individual wild animals. Organizations like Wild Animal Initiative are building the scientific foundation for this field, with $1 million funding multiple research projects on welfare assessment, academic partnerships advancing welfare biology, and policy frameworks for welfare-conscious wildlife management. While traditional conservation receives billions in funding from major foundations and government agencies, explicit wild animal welfare work receives only a few million dollars annually, making it a truly neglected area. However, the field faces significant challenges in identifying effective interventions due to ecological complexity, where well-intentioned actions may have unpredictable cascading effects across intricate natural systems. **For donors interested in potentially enormous scale but comfortable with building a field under uncertainty,** wildlife welfare offers an opportunity to shape an emerging area that could fundamentally transform how humans consider and address suffering beyond domesticated and farm animals, though success requires patience as the foundations continue to develop.

Climate Change: Climate philanthropy targets the threat of global warming through high-leverage interventions spanning clean energy development, transportation electrification, agricultural reform, forest preservation, policy advocacy, and climate justice. Organizations like the Good Food Institute and Clean Air Task Force demonstrate effective approaches, with $1 million in GFI funding critical research advancing alternative proteins that address the 15% of global emissions coming from animal agriculture. Despite growing commitments from major funders like the ClimateWorks Foundation, Bezos Earth Fund, and

Bloomberg Philanthropies, funding is disproportionately concentrated in developed countries on specific areas such as renewable energy and carbon tracking. The field faces significant challenges in attributing specific emissions reductions to particular interventions, demonstrating impact against the vast scale of global emissions, navigating long-term horizons for outcomes, and overcoming political opposition from vested interests. **For donors seeking systemic change with global implications, climate work offers potential for transformative impact,** though success requires comfort with complex causal chains and patience for gradual, cumulative progress.

Pandemic Preparedness and Prevention: Pandemic preparedness addresses catastrophic biological threats through a comprehensive approach that spans surveillance, research, capacity building, and policy development. COVID-19 demonstrated both the staggering potential harm (millions of deaths, trillions in economic damage) and critical gaps in existing systems. Organizations like the Johns Hopkins Center for Health Security exemplify high-impact work: $1 million can fund influential policy reports, simulation exercises, and response frameworks that directly shape governmental and international strategies. While the space attracts funding from major foundations like Gates, Coefficient Giving, and Rockefeller, alongside government agencies providing billions for research, support remains dangerously cyclical, typically surging after outbreaks but fading as public attention wanes. The field faces unique challenges in measuring effectiveness when success means "nothing happens," navigating fragmentation across global health and biosecurity domains, and overcoming political obstacles, including nationalism that hinders international cooperation. **For donors seeking impact on human welfare and future flourishing, pandemic work offers an opportunity to protect against threats that could destabilize civilization itself,** though success requires sustained commitment through periods when risks appear less salient.

High-Income Healthcare: High-income healthcare addresses health outcomes in wealthy nations through clinical interventions, mental health services, and preventive approaches; it focuses on non-communicable diseases, mental health conditions, and age-related disorders that dominate disease burden in developed countries. Organizations like Action for Happiness demonstrate innovative approaches: $1 million can fund courses teaching skills in happiness that reach thousands with 20–35% improvements in mental well-being scores, support hundreds of community groups, and develop digital resources accessed by millions. While the space attracts substantial funding from major foundations like the Robert Wood Johnson and Commonwealth Fund, alongside condition-specific funders, mental health receives disproportionately less support relative to its disease burden despite recent improvements. The field's primary limitation is cost-effectiveness. Interventions typically cost tens or hundreds of thousands of dollars per quality-adjusted life year gained compared to $50–200 in global health contexts, reflecting diminishing returns in already well-funded systems. **For donors prioritizing local impact within their own countries rather than maximizing global welfare, high-income healthcare offers meaningful opportunities to address critical gaps in mental health support and prevention,** though with significantly lower cost-effectiveness than interventions in developing regions.

High-Income Livelihoods: This type of philanthropy tackles economic opportunity challenges in wealthy nations through education, workforce development, entrepreneurship support, and structural barrier reduction, addressing technological disruption, inequality, declining mobility, and persistent disparities. Organizations like Year Up demonstrate meaningful impact: $1 million supports 40–50 underrepresented young adults through intensive skills training and corporate internships, generating validated 30–40% earnings increases ($7,000–8,000 annually) compared to control groups. While the space attracts substantial funding from major foundations like Lumina, Gates, Markle, and Strada, alongside billions in public investment, interventions typically show modest impacts at high per-participant costs. The field faces challenges in demonstrating cost-effectiveness compared to other philanthropic opportunities, attribution difficulties separating program effects from broader economic conditions, and a mixed evidence base where many common approaches deliver disappointing results in rigorous evaluations. **For donors prioritizing local economic impact in their own communities over global welfare maximization, high-income livelihoods offer opportunities to address critical gaps in economic mobility,** though with significantly lower cost-effectiveness than interventions in developing regions.

Human Services and Social Justice: This area addresses both immediate needs and systemic inequalities affecting marginalized populations through direct service provision and structural reform efforts. Organizations like the Equal Justice Initiative demonstrate this dual approach: $1 million can provide legal representation to dozens of individuals facing excessive punishments while simultaneously supporting research documenting systemic abuses, public education campaigns reaching millions, and policy advocacy that transforms laws affecting thousands. The space attracts diverse funding from major foundations like Ford, Open Society, and MacArthur, alongside community foundations and government contracts, though resources remain unevenly distributed. The field faces significant challenges in measuring the long-term impact of interventions addressing complex, multifaceted problems, with limited evidence bases and higher costs than health or economic interventions. Additionally, disagreements persist about prioritization, with most organizations taking a primarily local perspective focused on vulnerable groups within high-income countries or specific cities rather than applying a global welfare lens. **For donors prioritizing social equity and structural change alongside immediate suffering reduction, this area offers opportunities to address root causes of injustice,** though with greater uncertainty about measurable outcomes.

The Arts: Arts philanthropy supports creative expression across visual arts, music, literature, dance, theater, and film, aiming to preserve cultural heritage, foster creativity, expand educational opportunities, and increase accessibility for underserved communities. Organizations like Americans for the Arts and the National Endowment for the Arts demonstrate meaningful impact: $1 million can support dozens of community arts programs serving hundreds of participants, fund research documenting societal benefits, or provide operational support to cultural institutions in neglected areas; studies show programs can achieve 10–15% improvements in academic performance and up to 30% reduction in recidivism through prison arts initiatives. While the space attracts diverse funding from private foundations like Ford, Mellon, and Bloomberg, corporate foundations, public agencies, and community foundations, support remains geographically uneven, with rural and economically disadvantaged communities receiving disproportionately less. The field faces significant challenges in demonstrating objective impact compared to interventions with clear metrics like lives saved or income increased, alongside difficult ethical questions about prioritizing arts when more essential needs like food or healthcare remain unmet in many communities. **For donors who value cultural expression and its potential secondary benefits, arts funding offers opportunities to enrich communities**, though with greater uncertainty about comparative social value.

Overall, picking a cause area might be the most important way to narrow a scope. It can lead to a million dollars affecting a few or a few hundred lives. It's worth thinking deeply about what area you can make the most impact in and focusing on the area where you can make a real difference. Appendix G provides a deeper dive into each of the areas mentioned above.

Narrowing by Geographic Scope

Why the best location to focus on might be a place you have never thought of.

There are a hundred possible ways to narrow scope, and one of the first ways many grantmakers do so is by determining who is in their circle of concern: their moral circle, discussed earlier. If a grantmaker only cares about their city, that immediately limits the types of grants they will consider. Because of its concreteness, geographic narrowing is one of the best places to start thinking about scope.

If charity begins at home, the richest neighborhoods benefit most

Although philanthropy once embraced the notion that "charity begins at home," this sentiment has become less popular over time. In a world of extreme inequality and global challenges, a major concern has emerged: if charity begins at home, then the wealthiest neighborhoods end up reaping the greatest benefits.

More and more funders now recognize how problematic this is. The Gates Foundation, for instance, guided by the belief that "all lives have equal value," focuses on people and places with the most urgent needs, often far from its Seattle headquarters. This approach flips the old saying on its head: charity shouldn't begin at home. It should begin where it's needed most.

Ultimately, things like geographic proximity, similarity, or shared values shouldn't define the limits of our moral concern. Someone who looks, thinks, or lives differently still feels the same pain. If we can alleviate suffering, we should, regardless of how different the beneficiaries are from us or what caused their hardship.

The "veil of ignorance" is a thought experiment that gets at this idea. Imagine you didn't know who you would be born as. You could end up in any country, with any gender and ability level, or even as any animal species. What kind of world would you want to land in? What rules would feel fair? How would you want others to act?

It's a more global version than the golden rule to "treat others as you'd want to be treated," whoever and wherever they are. After all, most of what shapes our lives is luck. One of the strongest predictors of lifetime income is simply where you're born, a factor entirely beyond our control. If I could have been born anywhere, I'd want philanthropic funding to go where it can do the most good, not just to wherever the philanthropist happens to live.

Where in the world? How to choose a geographic focus

Having a geographic focus is common in the foundation world, and not just because of narrow moral circles. Whether close to home or far away, focusing on a particular region allows foundations to build a deeper understanding of the local culture, stakeholder landscape (e.g., governments, NGOs, funders, the private sector, and recipients), and dynamics. This can lead to stronger regional networks and better identification and vetting of grantmaking opportunities. However, foundations sometimes overemphasize the benefits of geographic familiarity relative to other important factors like the scale and tractability of the problems in that region.

Narrowing your foundation's scope to a specific location isn't essential. But if you decide that it is the right approach, make sure the area is narrow enough to allow for real specialization (e.g., "Asia" is likely too broad), but still large enough for impact at scale (e.g., "Fiji" or anywhere with under 10 million people may be too small for a large foundation). Keep in mind that once you choose a location, it can be hard to switch. Location-specific networks and skills are not often easily transferable.

If you do want to pick a geographic focus, it's a good idea to pick an option scoring relatively high on four factors: total need, incidence rate, neglectedness, and tractability. Most strong location candidates will probably score relatively high on all four, but a somewhat lower score on one may be acceptable as long as it doesn't pose a *limiting factor*, meaning something that may limit the effectiveness of targeted interventions. Let's break this down a bit:

- **Total need**: the number of potential beneficiaries in an area who stand to benefit from the types of interventions you plan to fund.

- In global health, for example, you can typically help the most people by working in regions with large populations affected by severe poverty and easily preventable health issues. An example is Kano State in Nigeria, which has a population of 16 million. Proportionately fewer people in need live in wealthier places such as New York, London, or Tokyo, and alleviating suffering in those settings is generally more challenging without substantial financial investment.

- However, total need alone isn't enough to guide your geography decision. If you only look at that, you're almost guaranteed to land on China, India, or Nigeria, countries with massive populations. The internal diversity of countries of this size means they often need to be approached at a state or regional level, and the scale of the problem in one region may actually be smaller than in other countries. In that sense, high diversity within a country can be a limiting factor.

- **Incidence rate:** the percentage of people or animals in a given population who experience (or will experience) the problem you are trying to solve. Low incidence rates combined with high total need suggest that although many people are affected overall, the problem is spread out, which may be a limiting factor.

- Conversely, high incidence but low total need may point to a very small location with limited opportunities for impact at scale (e.g., Lesotho or Samoa). In such cases, low total need can show up as a limiting factor, even when incidence is high.

- **Neglectedness**: how underserved the location is by foundations and government funding. Countries like the US may have relatively high maternal mortality (the highest among high-income nations), but they also benefit from advanced medical research systems, significant funding, and major international health collaborations.

  However, focusing solely on neglect can also be problematic. A country like the Democratic Republic of Congo might look promising across several dimensions, including neglectedness, but it is exceptionally difficult to operate in. That is why it's important to consider the final factor:

- **Tractability:** how easy or difficult it is to work in this geographic area successfully. Delivery of medical goods is a lot easier if there are roads between clinics.

As shown in the table below, a country may score highly on one dimension but poorly on another. If you choose to go down this path, it's essential to aim for relatively high scores across most criteria and to consider whether low scores in certain areas might cancel out the strengths in others.

Country	Total need	Neglectedness	Incidence rate	Tractability
Nigeria	High	Medium	High	Medium
DRC	High	High	High	Low
Bangladesh	Low	High	Low	High
US	Medium	Low	Low	High

Example: country comparison table for geographies in which to fund small-scale organizations focusing on global health

Country	Total Need (malaria burden)	Neglectedness (funding & attention)	Incidence Rate (cases per 1.000 per year)	Tractability (ease of intervention)
Nigeria	High (27% of global malaria deaths)	Medium (significant but uneven funding)	~300	Medium (net distribution works but challenges exist)
Democratic Republic of Congo (DRC)	High (2nd highest global burden)	High (conflict zones reduce access)	~350	Low (insecurity & logistics issues)
Bangladesh	Low (elimination phase, cases <10K/year)	High (historically underfunded)	<1	High (near elimination, focused interventions effective)
Peru	Medium (outbreaks in Amazon)	Medium (some public health focus)	~30	High (case detection & treatment work well)

Overall geographic scope can be a highly useful way to narrow down, particularly if your selected cause area is large enough to allow additional narrowing. Just remember that when picking a geographic scope, it's a choice that can be aimed at **impact** (e.g., picking a country that scores well on a table like above) or **convenience** (e.g., the country you are most familiar with or have a personal connection to). If you want to double your outcomes, it's best to **aim for impact.**

Once you have narrowed by cause area and geography, the final filter you can consider is NGO size.

Narrowing by NGO Stage

If you're tossing a ball with a child, what counts as a good throw depends a lot on the kid's age. What's impressive for a 5-year-old might be child's play for a 10-year-old. NGOs can vary in a similar way. The final method for narrowing scope we'll cover is based on the size and age of recipient organizations. This approach feels intuitive to many funders. A proposal from a brand-new organization seeking $50,000 will likely look very different from one submitted by a six-year-old organization asking for $5 million.

Similarly, the process you use to evaluate proposals and the criteria you prioritize can vary a lot depending on the size of the organizations you think are most promising. Focusing on grants or NGOs within a specific budget range can be an effective way to narrow what might otherwise feel like an overwhelming scope. For example, global poverty is a huge space, but if you limit your search to grants $100,000 or under in that area, it becomes far more manageable.

Different sizes of NGOs: the big tend to get the most

There are a few broad categories of NGO size that a foundation could choose to specialize in. Analogously to the for-profit world, foundations typically classify the stages of recipient organizations as seed, small, medium, or large, based on their annual budgets. These tiers roughly match those used by groups like DIV (Development Innovation Ventures) and the Global Innovation Fund (GIF).

Most NGOs are relatively small, with 92% operating on budgets under $1 million per year. But donations aren't spread evenly. A few large NGOs receive a disproportionate share of total funding.

Let's take a closer look at what it means to focus on each size tier, the pros and cons of doing so, and what those choices might imply for your grantmaking strategy.

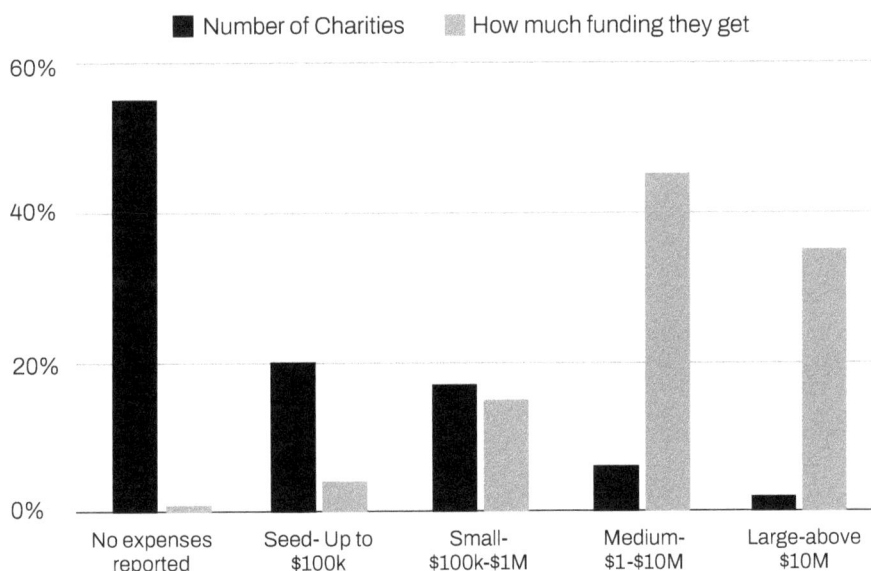

Comparing share of funding and number of charities by stage.[19]

Seed: An organization in its seed stage is typically very young; in many cases, you might be the organization's first funder. Seed-stage organizations usually have a founder or two and an idea, but little else beyond that. They typically operate on a shoestring, with a budget of less than $200,000. We also include pre-seed NGOs (e.g., those actively working on getting a new NGO started) in this category, as the same funders often cover these two sizes. The benefit of supporting an organization at the seed level is that your influence could mean the difference between a high-impact NGO getting founded or never even getting off the ground. The downside is that your investment carries a much higher risk. The vetting process for these organizations would focus more on the quality of the founders and the evidence-based, theory of change, and plans for the intervention than the specific NGO's track record.

Small: These are generally organizations with an annual budget under $1 million, often significantly less. A grant to NGOs in this range could be between $20,000 and $200,000. These organizations are typically quite young, typically under three years old, and have already begun to establish a track record. They may be looking to run a more formal pilot or test of their activities, but they will be characterized by a "we are still figuring this out" attitude and high flexibility to adapt and change compared to larger projects.

Supporting these small organizations can be exciting, as any extra resources they receive can have highly tangible and measurable results. Your support can mean the difference between them having to shut down, being mediocre, or becoming high-impact. Focusing your scope on small NGOs can give you the widest range of options to choose from and a higher possibility of finding neglected ones. As with seed-stage organizations, small NGOs carry more risk than larger ones but can be much more cost-effective.

Medium: Medium-sized organizations, typically aged three to 10 years, have established track records, making it easier to evaluate their past effectiveness. When you support them, you'll likely be one of many funders, as they often have multiple contributors backing annual budgets between $1 million and $10 million.

Investing in medium-sized organizations can strike a satisfying balance between reward and risk. But as you consider these larger recipients, a key question arises: are you truly making the most significant impact possible? If the organization could easily raise funding without your support, your resources might be better spent identifying and filling a gap elsewhere in the philanthropic landscape. And if you're not providing long-term support, will larger funders step in to sustain the work?

Large: In the realm of philanthropy, large organizations are the giants that often dominate the headlines (think Save the Children, Oxfam, BRAC, and the like). With operating budgets exceeding $10 million annually, these behemoths have typically been around for years, gradually expanding their reach to encompass a vast array of areas. Rarely does a single funder shoulder the entire financial burden of an organization at this scale; instead, support is typically spread across a diverse tapestry of individuals, foundations, and governments.

While large organizations are the most resilient and can absorb substantial funding, they are rarely as cost-effective as smaller organizations. Large organizations often undertake a wide range of interventions with varying levels of cost-effectiveness, making it challenging to selectively fund only the most effective ones.

Different strategies within size-scoping

There are four different, fairly common approaches that foundations use when deciding what size of NGO to focus on:

- Stay within your weight class
- Fill gaps within your cause area
- Smaller is better
- Size is not a big factor

Stay within your weight class: In this context, "weight class" means sticking with NGOs that are in roughly the same size range as your foundation. For example, if your foundation gives away $5 million a year, this might mean donating to NGOs with annual budgets between $0.5 million and $5 million, while skipping over very small or very large organizations outside that range.

This is the most common approach, largely because it's practical. If you're trying to move a lot of money, large grants are the easiest way to do it; if your funding is more limited, you tend to consider smaller ones. Psychologically, most foundations and grantmakers want to feel significant to the organization they are giving to, and so aim to make up 10% or more of the NGO's budget with a grant.

Weight class is a pretty good default and works well in many situations. But it can run into challenges in smaller contexts, particularly when there are a few very large funders but a relative dearth of smaller funders.

Fill gaps within your cause area: If you've already chosen a geography and cause area, you might be able to identify where in that philanthropic ecosystem funding is most needed. If your foundation is flexible, it could step in to fill a gap and improve the overall health of the ecosystem. The table below shows examples of where impact-focused funders might find underfunded spots, with green indicating gaps that are promising areas to focus on as of 2023. For example, this table suggests that, in terms of picking a size, it might make a lot more sense to focus on mid-stage funding for global health rather than the well-funded large-scale stage. Whereas for wildlife welfare, it might make more sense to focus on later-stage, more established, larger-scale funding gaps, as that is what is missing in that ecosystem.

Note that these are relative gaps. Cause areas are very differently funded, so comparisons should only be made within a cause area to get an idea of what NGO stages may offer higher impact opportunities.

Cause Area	Seed Funding (Under $100k / 2 years)	Small / Mid-stage Funding ($0.1M-1M / 2-5 years)	Medium / Growth Funding ($1M-$10M / 5-10 years)	Large-scale Funding ($10M+ / 10+ years)
Global Health	Middling	Limited	Middling	Very Strong
Global Income	Limited	Limited	Middling	Very Strong
Economic Growth	Middling	Strong	Strong	Middling
Artificial Intelligence	Middling	Strong	Middling	Very Strong
Farmed Animal Welfare	Strong	Middling	Middling	Strong
Wildlife Welfare	Middling	Middling	Limited	Limited
Climate	Middling	Strong	Strong	Very Strong
Pandemics	Limited	Middling	Strong	Strong
Mental Health	Middling	Limited	Middling	Middling
High School Education	Middling	Middling	Middling	Strong
Human Services	Strong	Strong	Strong	Middling
Arts	Middling	Middling	Strong	Very Strong

Smaller is better: Some foundations actively look for the smallest and youngest NGOs that meet their criteria. Newer organizations often give you more value per dollar, and a small grant can make a much bigger difference to them.

The tradeoff is that this approach is more time-consuming. Younger groups are harder to evaluate, and you'll need to fund more of them to deploy the same amount of capital. It's a riskier strategy that tends to involve more misses. It's also harder to find promising young organizations because they're often less networked, so foundations using this strategy tend to rely more on application processes that are open to anyone, which again take more time to evaluate.

Size is not a big factor: A final approach is to drop size constraints completely. This, of course, gives you the broadest range of options but also reduces your level of specialization. We think this makes particular sense for small cause areas, like pandemic preparedness in LMICs (Low- and Middle-Income Countries), where the total number of NGOs is already limited, and so size-based special-ization probably isn't feasible. If you've already narrowed your focus by geography or cause area, removing size as a filter is often the most sensible first step.

In sum: Size can be a useful tool to further narrow your scope, but it's highly dependent on how else you've already focused your search. The right strategy will depend on your foundation's context and goals.

Scope in a nutshell

- Most foundations do not pick a clear enough or narrow enough scope

- There are three common ways to narrow scope: geographic, cause area, or NGO size.

- Each of these methods can be used to help a grantmaker focus their attention and specialize in an area, allowing more impact to be created.

- Each can be examined through a lens of increasing impact, highlighting areas that are most commonly overlooked by other philanthropists. This allows not only more focus but also a focus on the scope that will have the most impact.

CHAPTER 2
POWERS

You can get 80% of the way to being a great grantmaker by using six principles well.

Why These 6 Principles?

At the start of the book, we introduced six principles (POWERS) that would be applicable regardless of the scope you chose. Here, we get to dive deeper into these concepts and learn why we picked them and how they can be applied in practice. The question "Why these six principles?" could go in three directions: why so few, why so many, and why these ones specifically?

Why so few? To be a perfect grantmaker, it would take hundreds of principles, concepts, and likely years of both study and practice. Our prior versions of this book were much longer, giving closer to 60 principles than six. But in practice, people tended to walk away with just 3–5 of the 60, often chosen at random, and not necessarily the most important ones. So, the question became: How much can we narrow (just like narrowing a scope) to get down to a more manageable number of principles that people can remember? We turned them into a handy acronym, POWERS, that makes them easy to remember. Plus, many more are included in the appendix of this book, and even more in our recommended reading.

Why so many? Honestly, fewer might have been better in many ways. For a while, we had five, which was about the most lessons grantmakers seemed to retain from a single book. But we added a sixth (the question of who should evaluate your grants) because it felt highly relevant to some (though not all) funders. And even if one doesn't apply to your situation, there's still a lot to get out of the book: each principle is designed to be broadly applicable, so it wouldn't be surprising if all six prove useful to any foundation.

Why *these* principles? Out of the many we considered, these were the most essential to the largest number of grantmakers. The six POWERS are directly connected to the biggest questions they had or the most common mistakes they made. We aimed to distill each principle into a single sentence, but they require their own chapters to understand the full reasoning behind them.

Here are the six principles that apply to funders regardless of scope, grant size, or grantmaking strategy.

- **Price tag:** Know what you're getting for your money
  (*What impact are you buying?*)

- **Options:** Don't pick until you've seen the menu
  (*Compare 10 or more options for every grant you give.*)

- **Who:** Pick the right judge for your grants
  (*Mini quiz: Who should evaluate them?*)

- **Evaluate:** Measure your grants by benchmarks, not vibes
  (*Compare each one to a proven NGO standard.*)

- **Reduce:** Give money, not homework
  (*Cap NGO time at 2 hours, plus 1 hour more per $50k granted.*)

- **Substance:** Don't fall for style over substance
  (*Focus on how the NGO actually works, not just how it presents itself.*)

Price Tag

You should know the price tag, and how much impact it buys, for every grant you give.

The toaster paradox: why we're better at buying appliances than funding charities

The $30 decision we take seriously

When Sarah needed a new toaster last month, she spent 20 minutes comparing models online: star ratings, customer reviews, brand reliability, and most importantly, whether it was worth the money. She'd never dream of clicking "Buy Now" without knowing if she was getting good value for $30 or accidentally paying $300 for the same thing. Yet last quarter, as a foundation program officer, she approved three grants totaling $1.2 million with far less comparative price data.

This isn't just Sarah's problem. It's a fundamental flaw in how the NGO sector operates. While we demand clear price-to-value relationships for everyday purchases, we've normalized making million-dollar charitable decisions with far less transparency around the amount of impact you are buying.

What are you actually buying?

The NGO marketplace has no Amazon. Open a browser to buy a toaster, and you'll immediately see which brands deliver the most value per dollar spent, with product images, ratings, reviews, and cost all laid out. Now try comparing an anti-malaria charity to a leadership development program or a community initiative. There's no easy way to tell which one delivers more value per dollar.

Most grant applications tell you how much money is being requested, but not what you're getting for that money. A $300,000 grant could create meaningful, measurable change, or it might achieve almost nothing. And the standard application format rarely forces that distinction.

What we're really after is cost-effectiveness: the value created relative to the resources invested. But in most grantmaking, that value is invisible. It's like walking into a store where the prices are all labeled, but the products are hidden behind a curtain. There are no reviews, no comparisons, and the only descriptions are written by the people selling the goods.

How big are the differences?

One of the biggest surprises in price tags and cost-effectiveness is just how wide the differences between options can be: often two to five times, and sometimes 100 times! Why such a big price gap? Partly because some NGOs are bloated, slow, or inefficient. But it can also come from much smaller things. An NGO that buys supplies in small quantities or uses overtrained staff to distribute them can easily end up spending three times more than it needs to.

In cases like that, the choice is clear: given the same outputs, almost everyone would pick the charity that delivers the same result at a lower price tag (i.e., more cost-effectively). But often the real differences come from taking a broader look at the goal. And the really big differences can come from stepping back and rethinking the goal itself. For example, shifting your focus from a single disease to broadly preventing causes of death can dramatically change the cost-effectiveness landscape. The chart below shows the large range of differences in the cost-effectiveness of global health interventions, with some areas being more than 20 times as effective, even working on the specific area of HIV treatment.

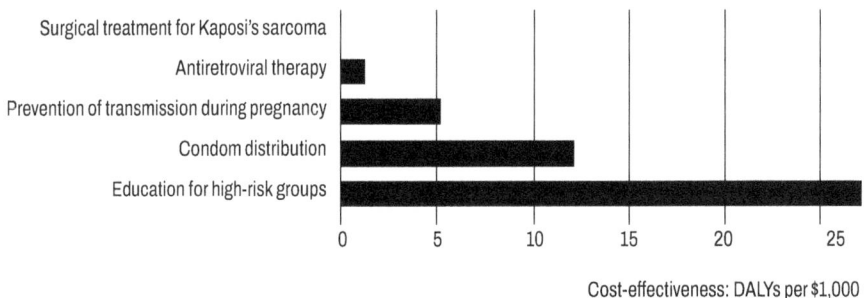

Cost-effectiveness: DALYs per $1,000

Cost-effectiveness of some HIV interventions

Is a fake price tag worse than none at all?

The annual report problem

Imagine walking into an electronics store where, instead of product descriptions and reviews, each appliance displays only the company's annual report: "Samsung: $189 billion revenue, 2.5 billion customers served." Would that help you decide whether this toaster is worth buying? Of course not.

Yet this exact scenario plays out daily in the nonprofit world. Organizations proudly announce, "Our NGO has saved 1 million lives with our $15 million budget." This creates the illusion of transparency. Just $15 per life saved sounds incredible! However, it masks a fundamental flaw: these are aggregate numbers, not marginal ones. You have no idea what your specific donation would accomplish.

Just like Samsung's total revenue tells you nothing about this toaster, an NGO's total budget-to-impact ratio hides the details: maybe one program saves lives for $5, while another costs $5,000. Unless you dig deeper, and unless you share the same definition of "life saved," you're just guessing.

The mystery box dilemma

Instead of misleading metrics, reality is often complete opacity. Picture ordering from Amazon based solely on a vague product description: "Samsung Box of Electronics: Might contain a toaster." You don't know what's inside. There's no itemized value, no reviews, no clarity. You just have to hope it's worth it.

That's how many charitable donations work in practice. Donors fund organizations with wide-ranging programs, some effective, some less so, without knowing where their money actually goes. Sometimes the NGO's own staff can't tell you exactly what specific initiatives actually accomplish.

In these cases, a vague or misleading cost-effectiveness claim can be worse than none at all. At least when no estimate is provided, you know you need to ask questions. A false sense of certainty (*"This NGO saves lives for just $15 each!"*) can stop donors from digging deeper. And that complacency fuels a funding ecosystem where rigorous measurement remains optional instead of essential.

When a price tag is done well, it becomes cost-effective

When Kelly purchased 500 textbooks for a low-income school, the invoice showed $15,000. But what did that money actually accomplish? Did students learn more? Did test scores improve? Did graduation rates increase? Without connecting costs to outcomes, we have a transaction, not an investment.

True cost-effectiveness bridges this gap. Rather than simply reporting "$30 per textbook distributed," meaningful measurement tells us "$157 per additional year of education" or "$1,890 per student who advances to higher education." This transformation from inputs to outcomes, using an outcome metric you are pursuing with your grantmaking, is what separates superficial transparency from genuine accountability.

Imagine if Amazon had researchers spending thousands of hours testing every toaster, tracking long-term performance, interviewing past buyers, and analyzing how each one is made. That's essentially what GiveWell does for charitable giving.

GiveWell: A charity comparison engine

While most charity evaluators settle for overhead ratios or emotional testimonials, GiveWell conducts exhaustive analyses that would make the most dedicated product reviewer blush. GiveWell researchers have been known to follow citation trails through multiple academic papers, contact field implementers directly, and commission independent studies, all to answer: *"How much good does each donated dollar do when given to charity X? And which charities will do the most with an extra dollar?"*

What matters is what we are buying and how confident we are in that outcome.

The result is something revolutionary in philanthropy: actual comparison shopping for impact. GiveWell's website displays charities with clear metrics of cost-effectiveness, such as:

- Malaria Consortium's seasonal malaria chemoprevention: $5,000 per life saved

- New Incentives vaccination program: $4,500 per life saved

- Helen Keller's vitamin A program: $3,500 per life saved

These are rigorously derived estimates based on program-specific interventions with clear causal pathways from donation to impact.

Going deeper: the price tag puzzle

Cost per what?

The endpoint matters more than the waypoint. True cost-effectiveness requires measuring outcomes (increased graduation rates, improved health, enhanced economic mobility) rather than outputs (people reached, services delivered, products distributed). The difference is profound, like choosing between a toaster advertised by "metal components used" vs. "perfectly browned toast produced."

The most rigorous philanthropic analyses break down costs into meaningful units:

- $3,500 per additional year of healthy life gained

- $850 per person lifted from extreme poverty

- $4,200 per additional high school graduate

These metrics connect money directly to mission, revealing the actual difference each dollar makes.

With cost-effectiveness, there is no "good enough"

Many philanthropists ask, "Is this charity cost-effective enough?" But this framing misses a crucial point: cost-effectiveness exists on a spectrum with no natural cutoff. Just as you'd prefer paying $15,000 rather than $20,000 for the same car, every improvement in philanthropic efficiency means more good accomplished per dollar.

The implications are profound. A charity that's twice as cost-effective doesn't just do a bit more good, but literally doubles the impact of every dollar. When effectiveness differences between interventions often span 10 times or 100 times, the opportunity cost of settling for "good enough" becomes significant.

What about marginal vs. average costs?

One tricky aspect of cost-effectiveness is that you're often funding just part of an organization's budget, typically the last part. That matters. NGOs tend to fund the most important and cost-effective work first, which makes sense. As a result, the average dollar given may look better than the next dollar you're considering giving.

Take a clean water charity with a $400,000 budget. The first $200,000 might serve easily accessible villages (cost: $10 per person). The next $100,000 reaches more remote areas (cost: $25 per person). The final $100,000 goes toward even harder to reach areas (cost: $50 per person). If you donate $10,000 after the first $400,000 has been deployed, instead of buying at the average cost of impact, you're buying at the margin, and that marginal cost is $50 per person.

Weaknesses of cost-effectiveness

Cost-effectiveness estimates are predictions, not guarantees. Models can contain errors or optimistic assumptions. The best philanthropists embrace this uncertainty while still recognizing the value of imperfect information.

When the differences between interventions are 10 times or 100 times, even rough estimates provide crucial guidance. Would you rather support a program that saves lives for around $4,000 each or one that costs closer to $400,000 per life saved? Even with a lot of uncertainty in the numbers, the direction of the decision is usually clear.

Right-sizing your time spent on cost-effectiveness

The bigger the grant, the more important it is to get a more reliable number. The resources devoted to cost-effectiveness analysis should scale with the stakes:

- $1,000–$20,000 grants: Back-of-the-envelope estimates to check if it's likely worth it.

- $20,000–$200,000: Detailed spreadsheet models with another set of eyes to double-check.

- $200,000+: Consider commissioning external research or collaborating with other funders to build a high-quality model.

Snapshot summary

Understanding and valuing what a grant actually buys might be the single best way for a grantmaker to increase their impact. At the end of the day, there will always be more problems than dollars to solve them, so we have to be frugal and thoughtful with our giving. Every grant should come with a price per benefit or a cost-effectiveness estimate, showing how many people are helped per dollar, and by how much. This makes cross-comparison possible and ultimately leads to better grantmaking.

We care about price and value in most purchases we make, and with such big differences in price tags and cost-effectiveness in grantmaking, knowing the numbers can be the difference between saving one life and saving many.

How to apply this in your grantmaking

1. Request cost-effectiveness analyses (CEAs) from your potential grantees. If they are not familiar with the term, ask for the information you would need to fill out the form on the next page (e.g., exactly how many beneficiaries will be helped and in what way for the extra funding you are providing).

2. Check if there are existing CEAs of similar interventions, as this will substantially help your evaluation.

3. For larger grants, decide who will lead on cost-effectiveness. This might mean building your own skills in cost-effectiveness analysis, or bringing in an external researcher or advisor. (Keep this in mind when reading the "Who Should Do Your Grantmaking" chapter.)

4. When conducting a CEA or asking someone else to do one, state the main assumptions and uncertainties and how changes in those would affect the cost-effectiveness.

5. Sense-check your CEA model with another grantmaker or staff member.

Activity: create a simple cost-effectiveness estimate for a grant

We can do a quick CEA, using the table below.

Step	Description
NGO name	(Insert name of the organization.)
A) Annual NGO budget	If you have an annual budget from the NGO, use that. Otherwise, try to estimate the costs on your own.
B) Number of beneficiaries	Number of people or animals directly helped by the NGO over the course of a year.
C) Select an impact metric	Choose a metric that allows comparisons across NGOs (e.g., lives saved, DALYs averted, income gained).

D) Estimate impact per beneficiary on that metric *	Estimate the average impact *per beneficiary* using your chosen metric (e.g., if 1 in 100 people are saved, the impact per person = 0.01 lives saved). These estimates are often found in NGO annual reports.
E) Calculate impact	Multiply B × D to get the total impact (e.g., 1,000 people × 0.01 = 10 lives saved).
F) Calculate the cost per unit of impact	Divide the budget (A) by total impact (E) to get cost-effectiveness (e.g., $100,000 ÷ 10 lives = $10,000 per life saved).

*The hardest step in this chart is often D: How much is a beneficiary helped by the intervention? If you are struggling with this, consider changing the metric to something easier to estimate. For example, if all the charities you are comparing hand out reading glasses, you could calculate a cost per pair of reading glasses handed out instead of, say, the income created from more reading glasses. However, a better long-term solution is getting the numbers directly from your grantee. Caring about how many beneficiaries are helped, how much each one benefits, and knowing the price tag/budget is the only way to get a cost-effectiveness estimate.

Options

Compare 10 or more options for every grant you give.

What small restaurant menus have in common with grantmaking

Imagine you're at a restaurant with only two items on the menu: a mediocre sandwich and a slightly better salad. No matter how brilliant you are at making decisions, the best meal you'll get is that slightly better salad.

> *"The goal shouldn't be to make the perfect decision every time but to make fewer bad decisions than everyone else."*
>
> —Spencer Fraseur[20]

The power of option creation

What truly separates exceptional grantmakers from average ones isn't just decision-making skill but creating a rich menu of options to decide between in the first place. This idea is surprisingly counterintuitive, yet undeniably concrete: you can only choose grants as good as your best option.

Think about it this way. Choosing between two options means your ceiling is the better of the two grants. Choosing among 10 carefully vetted options? Your ceiling just got dramatically higher. Selecting from 100 rigorously selected opportunities? Now you're playing an entirely different game.

Finding the sweet spot matters. Reviewing 1,000 grants in depth to award just one would crush both grantmakers and applicants under mountains of paperwork. The magic range appears to be 10 to 100 grants reviewed for each one funded. A typical open funding round might attract 300 applications with five grants awarded (a 60:1 ratio), well within this optimal zone.

The surprising mistake most funders make

It might be counterintuitive, but the real problem is a scarcity of standout options, more than an overflow of applications.

When funders rely exclusively on personal referrals, closed application processes, or narrow networks, they quietly cap their own impact. Even the sharpest decision-maker can't do much with a limited menu.

It is worth asking yourself if you are really seeing enough genuinely promising options? Or are you just picking the best from a list that's far too short?

Filling your grant pipeline: the power of public rounds

We just covered how limited options can constrain good grantmaking. So how do strategic grantmakers find more (and better) ones?

When the Gates Foundation launched its Grand Challenges initiative with an open request for proposals, they didn't just tap into their existing network. They opened applications worldwide and discovered breakthrough solutions from researchers they'd never heard of in countries they rarely funded. The result? Game-changing innovations in global health that their traditional networks might never have surfaced.

Public rounds don't just add more options; they also increase your ceiling. They break through the invisible barriers of your existing network, bringing in perspectives, approaches, and solutions that challenge your assumptions about what's possible.

The network multiplier: leverage other people's networks

Every grantee you've funded is connected to dozens of other promising organizations that you've never heard of. Other funders in your space collectively know hundreds of candidates you haven't yet discovered.

The Robin Hood Foundation mastered this approach. After each funding cycle, they systematically ask: "Who else should we know about?" This simple question has unlocked access to grassroots organizations deeply embedded in communities they aim to serve.

Think of each contact as a potential multiplier. When semiconductor pioneer Andy Grove was asked the secret to Intel's success, he said: "We let each person's network become Intel's network." Smart grantmakers apply the same principle, systematically harvesting the collective knowledge of everyone they interact with.

Tracking down the best

The best opportunities rarely arrive conveniently packaged on your doorstep. They must be hunted down, uncovered, and sometimes created through deliberate prospecting.

Remember that the quality of your decisions will never exceed the quality of your options. Are you actively expanding your menu, or just choosing from the same limited selection?

Decision tools: how smart grantmakers compare apples to oranges

Once you have enough options, the real comparison can begin. Imagine you're judging the finale of a talent show. Five performers have just given it their all, and now you have to pick a winner. But how do you compare a world-class violinist to a dazzling dancer or a mind-blowing magician?

The spreadsheet superpower: Weighted Factor Models

When NASA engineers needed to decide which materials would protect astronauts during reentry, they didn't rely on gut feeling. They built a decision matrix, or what grantmakers call a Weighted Factor Model (WFM).

At its core, a WFM is a structured comparison tool that turns subjective judgments into quantifiable numbers. Each row represents a different grant option, and each column reflects the criteria that matter most to you: impact potential, team strength, cost-effectiveness, or anything else you care about.

You can then calculate an overall score by multiplying each criterion's score by its percentage weighting. See the examples for Grant A and Grant B below:

(A simple weighted factor model)

Grant name	Overall score	Cost-effectiveness	Strength of team	Strength of idea	Evidence	Strength of execution
Weighting	*100%*	*30%*	*20%*	*20%*	*20%*	*10%*
Grant A	8.1/10	9/10	8/10	8/10	7/10	8/10
Grant B	6.3/10	8/10	6/10	7/10	4/10	5/10

WFMs shine in the critical window when you're comparing about four to 20 options, a range where most grantmakers struggle. The framework functions as a transparency machine, requiring you to state exactly why Grant A outranks Grant B on organizational strength or theory of change.

WFMs work best when you already have decent information on each option and need to make fine-grained distinctions between a number of reasonably strong candidates.

The courtroom method: 3x3 decision making

While judges use scales of justice as a symbol, the best legal minds actually use something closer to a 3x3 framework to systematically weigh evidence for and against each position.

The 3x3 method excels when you're down to your final round, typically two to four options that you understand deeply. Rather than reducing everything to numbers, it creates a structured conversation around strengths and weaknesses.

A simple template for 3x3 decision making

Comparison Table	
Grant option 1: Grant A	**Grant option 2: Grant B**
Pros 1. Cost-effectiveness outstanding 2. Pretty solid on everything else 3. Recommendation from person Y, who has similar values to me	Pros 1. Cost-effectiveness great 2. Theory of Change pretty strong, and another policy idea fits my portfolio
Cons 1. Cost-effectiveness relies on many assumptions 2. Evidence base mostly refers to African countries, intervention is in Asia	Cons 1. Evidence base pretty weak—novel policy intervention 2. Team only just got together and is new to the GHD space
Key factor Check if intervention is likely to replicate in Asia at the same cost-effectiveness, maybe not a huge problem Maybe a better fit for foundation ABC?	**Key factor** Look for evidence on similar policy interventions, ask person Y for advice; otherwise, the lack of evidence may be quite worrying Perhaps give advice to the team on execution plans— connect to mentor in the space?

The power of this approach lies in its ability to force intellectual honesty. When it's properly executed, you must acknowledge that even your favorite grant has drawbacks. (If you can't find any weaknesses in your top pick, you're wearing rose-colored glasses!)

You may soon experience a common revelation. The brilliant, world-changing proposal you liked suffers from one critical weakness: it's not neglected. Other funders have already spotted its brilliance and are lining up with checkbooks open.

The hidden truth about all decision tools

Grants are rarely "good" or "bad" in absolute terms. They're just better or worse compared to your other options. Even Einstein might finish last in a beauty pageant, while a randomly chosen supermodel could struggle in a physics competition.

The right decision tool doesn't make the choice for you, but it makes your thinking visible, allowing you to see exactly how your values and judgments are driving the outcome. That process alone can make you better at grantmaking.

The grantmaker who gets ambushed

It was getting late, and the hotel bar was nearing closing time when I sat next to Bill. He was a fellow grantmaker I knew, and he looked as if he'd just survived an apocalypse—exhausted and slightly traumatized after a long day at the conference.

"All day, people have been approaching me for money. Someone even waited outside the bathroom for me to come out so they could pitch," Bill moaned, his voice carrying a bit too far in the half-empty bar where conference attendees were still nursing their drinks.

"Why would they do that? How do you normally pick who to give grants to?" I asked, genuinely curious since we'd never discussed his methods in detail.

Bill shifted uncomfortably before confessing, "Oh, well, normally I meet people at conferences and fund the people I like best."

No wonder Bill felt hunted. As our conversation deepened, I discovered his entire grantmaking strategy resembled a game of chance: conferences and referrals from current grantees were his only pipelines for finding new organizations to fund. Bill had unwittingly created an environment where the optimal strategy for NGOs was to ambush him outside restrooms (and yes, he actually funded that persistent bathroom stalker's project).

The most alarming revelation was that Bill only seriously evaluated one or two applicants for every grant he awarded. He'd substituted inaccessibility for actual vetting, believing that by making himself difficult to reach, only the most worthy would break through. In reality, this approach backfired spectacularly. Rather than finding the most impactful organizations, he was merely funding the most persistent ones or those privileged enough to afford conference tickets, hotel rooms, and cross-country flights.

What Bill desperately needed wasn't a bodyguard but a system. With a structured application process and transparent method for getting on his radar, he could transform his conference experience from an exhausting game of hide-and-seek to the productive networking opportunity other grantmakers enjoyed with their grantees.

The grantmaker whose homework gets copied

The next morning at the same conference, I spoke with Jack, another grantmaker from my professional circle who represented the polar opposite of Bill's approach. Though equally well-known and frequently approached for funding, Jack moved through the conference with relaxed confidence.

Jack had built a fortress of process where Bill had only barricades. Everyone in the sector understood Jack's methodology. While they could certainly introduce themselves at conferences, potential grantees knew the real work involved a structured follow-up call, thorough due diligence review, and collaborative discussion with their team members.

Unlike Bill's handful of annual grants with minimal comparison, Jack awarded dozens, while deliberately evaluating 20 additional possibilities for each one funded. His foundation operated from a clear model with defined benchmarks, allowing him to weigh every proposal against consistent criteria while staying mindful of both his budget and how many organizations met the bar.

Jack's foundation had built a respected process and an approach so effective that other funders routinely asked to copy their application forms and structured interview questions. His genuine curiosity and encyclopedic knowledge of major grantmakers and NGOs made him a natural connector, often spearheading coordination efforts across multiple funding networks in his cause area.

While comparing Jack and Bill might initially seem unfair given Jack's larger team and budget, their radically different conference experiences stemmed primarily from their processes, not their resources. Jack would depart with a robust spreadsheet of carefully cataloged options to evaluate thoroughly, while Bill left exhausted, his grantmaking decisions shaped largely by the random chance of who managed to corner him between sessions. Jack also left a lot happier and more refreshed, the conference being energizing instead of draining, as it was for Bill.

Deeper dive: two ways to improve your decisions

Let's go for another food-based metaphor. Imagine you're a chef with just two ingredients versus one with a fully stocked pantry. Who's going to whip up the better meal? Making good decisions works the same way in grantmaking and beyond. It comes down to having more options to choose from and more criteria to judge them by. We've noticed that the best decision-makers lean hard on both, and that these vary a lot between funders. So, to improve your decisions, try these two things:

1. Consider more options before deciding.

2. Consider more criteria to evaluate options.

More options: breaking free from option ignorance

The difference between exceptional and mediocre decision-makers often boils down to how many possibilities they explore before committing. Most of us instinctively grab the first promising grant opportunity that crosses our desk and decide to either fund it fully or not at all. Yet something remarkable happens when we challenge ourselves to generate 10 alternatives: we frequently discover several options superior to our initial considerations.

This pattern repeats itself across the grantmaking landscape. When only two options exist—fund or don't fund—decisions become binary and simplistic. But when multiple possibilities emerge, nuanced solutions appear:

Basic Approach: Low Options + Simple Thinking

- Grant One: Yes/No

- Grant Two: Yes/No

Intermediate Approach: More Options + Convergent Solutions

- Grant One:
    - Full funding of the current request
    - Partial funding
    - No funding
    - Grant Two:
    - Full funding of current request
    - Partial funding
    - No funding
- Grants Three through Seven (similar options)

Advanced Approach: Multiple Options + Divergent Solutions

- Grant One:
    - Multi-year full funding
    - Full funding for the current year only
    - Explore co-funding opportunities with partners
    - Partial funding with specific conditions
- Grant Two:
    - Quickly decline without feedback
    - Decline with detailed feedback for next round
    - Decline with referrals to three better-matched funders
- Grants Three through Seven (with similarly detailed options)

The advanced approach consistently delivers greater impact by recognizing that grantmaking doesn't happen in isolation. Funders often possess stronger connections within the philanthropy community than NGOs themselves, creating tremendous value through thoughtful matchmaking with appropriate funders, especially those with closed application processes.

Within our funder networks, we regularly discuss the ecosystem implications of each grant: how might this decision affect others in the same space, and what precedent it sets for our funding community.

More criteria: expanding your decision-making lenses

"It is important to draw wisdom from many different places. If we take it from only one place, it becomes rigid and stale."

—Iroh, *Avatar: The Last Airbender*

We've talked a lot about expanding your options, such as adding more grants to compare and more ways to use applications. This next section is about something else: expanding the number of ways you evaluate each grant. In other words, how to make those decision-making models deep and nuanced enough to actually give you useful data.

Would you trust a doctor who only checked your temperature before diagnosing you? Of course not, and the same goes for grantmaking. No single metric, tool, or worldview gives you the full picture. Each one has blind spots. The strongest decisions come from looking through multiple lenses. When a grant holds up well across the board and really shines in a few key areas, that's when you know you've got something great.

It's time to get creative in considering options

Consider this comparison for a seemingly simple decision: Should I attend the (fictional) Impactful Philanthropy Conference (IPC)?

Weak analysis: two-dimensional thinking

Pros	Cons
It's a fairly important event.	It will cost significant time.
I get significant value from events like this.	It will cost significant money.
Few people with similar views get invited, so I could have a lot of leverage.	Maybe someone else could cover the same ground.

This quick assessment feels efficient, but it lacks depth. By contrast, the expanded analysis below takes more time up front but dramatically improves decision quality by uncovering key factors that might otherwise stay hidden. It also surfaces a crucial question: what are the real cruxes of this decision? Not all pros and cons are equal. Often, just one or two make or break the choice.

Strong analysis: multi-dimensional thinking

Pros	Cons
Direct	**Direct**
It's a fairly important event.	It will cost significant time.
I get significant value from events like this.	It will cost significant money.
Historically, these types of events have been worth the use of time for my foundation.	Last year, it seemed like there were a lot of promising leads, but there was a high flake-out rate.
For my foundation	**For my foundation**
It likely makes us seem more cooperative.	It may associate my foundation with views we don't support.
Probably positive for our relationships with key actors.	
	For IPC
	This area is a less important space for us now.
For IPC	
Few people with similar views get invited, so I could have a lot of leverage.	Some of the other attendees raise reputation concerns for us.
If we don't go, even fewer people who share similar priorities may get invited in the future.	**Opportunity cost**
	This year, more people from our network got invited, so the extra value is lower?
Opportunity cost	Maybe a colleague could cover the same ground?
More people from our network got invited, which could increase the extra value?	
How many people would both be 1) useful to chat to and 2) I could not set up a remote call with easily instead?	

Key factors or cruxes
1. Can a colleague cover enough of the same ground?
2. Do we generally want to move towards or away from this sphere of actors?
3. How many people would it be 1) useful to chat to and 2) easy to set up a remote call with instead?

Even for seemingly straightforward decisions, examining the situation from three to five perspectives instead of just one or two creates a decision-making superpower. With practice, generating these additional considerations becomes both faster and more intuitive.

Snapshot summary

Great grantmaking isn't about perfect decision-making; it's about creating a rich menu of high-quality options before you decide. Just as a chef with only two ingredients can't create a masterpiece regardless of skill, even the most brilliant grantmaker can't fund exceptional projects if they're not in the selection pool. The most successful funders maintain a selection ratio of 10-100 options for every grant awarded, using open application processes that break through network boundaries and systematically leverage relationships to discover hidden gems.

Once you've assembled your menu of possibilities, structured comparison tools transform subjective judgments into meaningful evaluations. Whether using a weighted factor model for comparing multiple candidates or a 3x3 pros/cons framework for finalist decisions, these approaches make your thinking visible and force intellectual honesty about each option's strengths and weaknesses. The most powerful insight? Grants are rarely "good" or "bad" in absolute terms; they're better or worse compared to your alternatives.

Is your grantmaking strategy more like Bill's (hunted at conferences, making reactive decisions) or Jack's (confidently exploring systematically vetted options)? Your answer affects not just who gets funded, but the quality of your impact and your professional experience. Start today: gather 10 or more options for your next grant decision, evaluate them across at least five different criteria, and watch how quickly your ceiling for excellence rises above what you thought possible.

Activity: compare three grants

In this activity, you'll directly compare three grants. It works best if all three are on the edge of being fundable. For example, three middle-ground options rather than one obvious yes, one obvious no, and one maybe. Start with the more narrative 3x3 model: list pros, cons, and key factors for each. This approach often reveals patterns and can help clarify your thinking. Then, if helpful, you can translate your insights into a more numbers-based WFM. Neither method is perfect, but together, they're useful tools for seeing where each grant stands out or falls short.

A simple template for 3x3 decision making

Comparison table		
Grant option 1:	**Grant option 2:**	**Grant option 3:**
Pros 1. 2. 3.	Pros 1. 2. 3.	Pros 1. 2. 3.
Cons 1. 2. 3.	Cons 1. 2. 3.	Cons 1. 2. 3.
Key factors	Key factors	Key factors

A simple weighted factor model

Grant name	Cost-effectiveness (30%)	Team strength (20%)	Idea strength (20%)	Evidence (20%)	Execution (10%)	Overall score — out of 100
						.

Who

Who should research and decide on your grants?

Why you might not be the best person to evaluate your own grants

---

The phone buzzed with another meeting reminder. Jessica stared at it, feeling overwhelmed. As the newly appointed director of her family's foundation, she faced hundreds of grant applications, dozens of cause areas, and had limited time to make thoughtful decisions. Her background in finance had prepared her for many challenges, but not this one: *Who* should actually evaluate these grants?

Should she hire staff? Work with advisors? Join a funding circle? Or tackle it all herself?

Grantmaking is a hard job. Choosing between hundreds of applications, conducting research, interviewing candidates, and evaluating outcomes requires significant time and expertise. Like any profession, you can excel or struggle at it, and experience makes a profound difference in your effectiveness.

Depending on your resources and interests, grantmaking might be a part-time hobby, a full-time job, or even require multiple staff members. The approach that works best depends on your unique situation and preferences.

Before we dive into the options, here's an uncomfortable truth: even if you're smart and well-intentioned, you might not be the best person to evaluate all your own grants. Here's why:

1. **Expertise and interest gaps:** Most people don't have deep knowledge across all the fields they'll need to understand in order to be great grantmakers.

2. **Time constraints**: Thorough evaluation requires a significant time investment.

3. **Feedback limitations**: It's hard to assess your own effectiveness, and almost no one will tell you if your grantmaking is weak.

The good news? The philanthropic ecosystem offers multiple solutions to address these challenges. Below is a quick quiz to help determine which approach might work best for your situation.

Who should evaluate the grants? Grantmaking approach quiz

Instructions: Answer the five questions below. Each one will point you toward certain grant-making approaches that might suit you better than others. At the end, you'll find instructions on how to use your answers to figure out which evaluation method, or combination of methods, might be the best fit for you right now.

1. How much time can you realistically dedicate to grantmaking?

Think about Jade, who originally planned to manage all her grantmaking herself while keeping her full-time finance job. But after tracking her time for a month, she realized she only had about five hours a week to spend on philanthropy.

A. 35+ hours a week: Grantmaking will be my full-time job

  • Hiring foundation staff

  • Do it yourself

  • Test out multiple options

B. 10-35 hours a week: Grantmaking will be a part-time job

  • Hiring foundation staff

  • Do it yourself

  • Deploy via a funding circle (see below)

  • Test out multiple options

C. 2-10 hours a week: Grantmaking will be my No. 1 hobby

- Deploy via a funding circle

- Philanthropic advisor

D. 0-2 hours a week: Grantmaking will be one hobby among others

- Philanthropic advisor

- Deploy by giving to other funds

- Charity evaluators

2. What is your annual grantmaking budget?

Consider Michael, who inherited $200,000 and wanted to donate it effectively. Given his modest budget relative to most foundations ($1 million–$100 million per year), he quickly realized that hiring staff would consume most of his philanthropy dollars in administrative costs. This clarity helped him focus on more appropriate options.

A. >$5,000,000

- Hiring foundation staff

- Test out multiple options

B. $5,000,000 > $100,000

- Philanthropic advisor

- Funding circles

C. < $100,000

- Charity evaluators

- Funds

- Do it yourself

- Rules out most funding circles

3. Do you value your grantmaking having a social aspect?

Elena found herself energized by collaborative decision-making. When she joined a funding circle, her enthusiasm for philanthropy grew exponentially because she enjoyed the community discussions. Meanwhile, her brother preferred making decisions independently after consulting with experts. Both were effective, but in different contexts that matched their temperaments.

A. Yes, the more people, the better

- Funding circle
- Hiring foundation staff

B. I prefer one-on-one social grantmaking

- Philanthropic advisor
- Charity evaluators
- Funds

C. No, I want to do it myself

- Funds
- Charity evaluators
- Do it yourself

D. Not sure

- Test out multiple options

4. Do you lean toward higher-risk, high-upside grants or prefer more certainty about a grant's impact?

David, a tech entrepreneur, brought his comfort with uncertainty and big potential payoffs to his philanthropy. He preferred funding promising but unproven interventions, making funding circles for earlier-stage projects a natural fit. His wife, Sarah, a physician, valued evidence and predictability, leading her to prefer charity evaluators for her portion of their giving.

A. Preference for higher certainty

- Charity evaluators
- Funds
- Hiring foundation staff

B. Unclear/unsure

- Philanthropic advisor
- Test out multiple options

C. Preference for higher risk and higher returns

- Funding circle
- Do it yourself

5. Does your cause area limit your options?

When Priya wanted to support global health, she discovered that several specialized evaluators existed in that space. This made her decision easier compared to her interest in supporting global education, where she found fewer structured evaluation resources.

A. Does it have a charity evaluator (climate, animals, global health, global livelihoods/income as of 2025)?

- If no: -4 points to charity evaluators

B. Does it have a funding circle (global health, animals, biorisk, income, mental health, and effective altruism as of 2025)?

- If no: -2 points to funding circle

C. Some of my areas do, but others do not

- +1 to all options

D. Unsure about my cause area

- Philanthropic advisor
- Test out multiple options

E. Not sure

- Do it yourself
- Hiring foundation staff
- Philanthropic advisor

Which approach fits you best?

For each approach, count the number of questions where the approach was included as a viable option in your answer. Total them up to identify which options might be most promising for you. You can read the short descriptions for all the options below, but we recommend digging into the one-pagers for your top two highest-scoring approaches on the following pages. They're worth the extra time.

For example, if you answer C in question one, you add one point to both funding circles and philanthropic advisor. You answer B in question two, and add two more points to the same. You answer A in question three, giving a point each to funding circles and hiring staff. And so forth.

Score	Approach	Short description
	Charity evaluators	If you like higher certainty options or have minimal time, a charity evaluator might be a great fit for you. They often do highly in-depth research, but only work in a select number of areas.
	Funds	Funds are essentially a lighter version of charity evaluators. They cover a larger range of areas, but often with less depth and transparency.
	Funding circle	A funding circle is a good option when a grantmaker has a moderate budget, values the social aspect of collaborative grantmaking, has a moderate or high degree of expertise and time to dedicate, and can accept a higher degree of variability in impact.
	Philanthropic advisor	A flexible way to boost your decision-making with minimal time or money. Great if you're not big enough for full-time staff but still want that level of insight.
	Foundation staff	Likely the most intense and high-cost option, but also the way to get the most original hours of work on a project. This makes sense for larger foundations that have an appetite for exploring new areas and are happy to dedicate themselves to this for a certain amount of time (1+ years).
	Do it yourself	A good fit if you have lower monetary resources but more time. Being connected to a community is especially important since grantmaking can be isolating.
	Test out multiple options	If this scores highest, you likely have some major uncertainties to resolve before selecting a strategy. Consider testing your next 2-3 top options before committing long-term.

Charity evaluators

What is a charity evaluator? Charity evaluators are organizations that assess and rate the effectiveness and impact of charitable organizations. Their aim is to provide donors with objective, evidence-based information to guide their giving decisions. Typically, they have a small set of top recommended charities and go super deep into a narrow cause area.

Benefits of using a charity evaluator:

- Offers objective analysis of a charity's evidence base, cost-effectiveness, and leadership.

- Gives concrete comparative ratings of charities within the same cause area.

- Very large staffing teams (GiveWell has more than 50 staff and puts in about 60,000 hours of research each year) allow for extremely in-depth research.

- The best charity evaluators are highly transparent in their methodology, so you can see how and why they came to the conclusions they did.

When to use a charity evaluator:

- You want your donations to have the greatest possible impact, but don't have the time or expertise to thoroughly research charities yourself.

- You want to compare charities working in the same space to identify the best giving opportunities, and there is a charity evaluator in that space.

- You want to donate to options that are highly likely to do high levels of good.

- You are skeptical of most charities but only have time to spot-check a few.

The charity evaluation space has evolved considerably in recent years. While early evaluators often focused heavily on financial metrics like overhead ratios, the best modern evaluators employ sophisticated frameworks drawing from economics and medicine.

Some recommended charity evaluators: Below are some well-regarded charity evaluators. However, different evaluators employ different methodologies and may be more or less aligned with your values and priorities, so it's worth exploring several to find the best fit. GiveWell uniquely stands out as the first and largest of these charity evaluators, with many others being founded based on its example.

Some recommended charity evaluators

Philanthropic funds

What is a philanthropic fund? This is a vehicle for pooling capital from multiple donors to support a specific cause area or set of organizations. Funds are typically managed by a team with expertise in the focus area, which is responsible for sourcing and evaluating giving opportunities. They fall somewhere between a charity evaluator and a funding circle.

Benefits of a philanthropic fund:

- Lets you support a cause without needing to build deep expertise or connections in the space.

- Pools capital from multiple donors to make larger, game-changing grants.

- Opens the door to backing higher-risk, higher-reward opportunities that individual donors or charity evaluators might pass on. (Many evaluators offer a built-in fund for this purpose.)

When to use a philanthropic fund:

- You want to support a specific cause but don't have the time or expertise to find the best opportunities yourself.

- You trust the fund's team to have strong credibility and deep expertise in the focus area.

- You'd like to pool resources with other donors to back larger, higher-leverage projects.

- You have limited time, a higher risk appetite, or there is no charity evaluator working in your space.

Some well-run example funds:

Agency Fund[21]: A multi-donor collaborative unified around a singular vision to invest in ideas and organizations that expand human agency. You can join the pooled fund or selectively co-invest alongside it. AF can also issue joint calls where your strategic objectives align with its approach.

Effective altruism funds: Animal welfare fund[22]: The EA Animal Welfare Fund's mission is to alleviate the suffering of non-human animals globally through effective grantmaking. The fund's grants portfolio prioritizes interventions that can collectively have the highest impact and help the greatest number of animals.

Bloom Wellbeing Fund[23]: This fund focuses on enabling minds around the world to bloom. It identifies and supports nonprofit organizations viewed as doing pioneering work, helping them to scale their missions to improve lives. This fund focuses on well-being, so grants are aimed at creating that measurably and cost-effectively, and reducing suffering at scale.

Funding circles

What is a funding circle? A funding circle is a collaborative network of philanthropists and foundations that focus their giving on a specific cause area—like global health, animal welfare, or early-stage nonprofits. These groups typically aim to stay around the size of a dinner party rather than a conference, fostering high levels of trust and close collaboration among members.

The level of coordination within funding circles can vary significantly. Some circles share application processes and funding pools, conduct joint due diligence, and make collective grant decisions. Other larger circles maintain looser affiliations, sharing information and perspectives through informal communication channels but making independent funding choices.

Benefits of a funding circle:

- Improve coordination by facilitating information-sharing and comprehensive coverage of funding gaps and opportunities.

- Simplify fundraising for nonprofits by providing a streamlined application process.

- Expand awareness of promising organizations and interventions for grantmakers.

- Provide a rewarding experience of learning and community for participants.

When to use a funding circle:

- **You have a moderate budget.** Funding circles work well for donors who have enough funding to meaningfully contribute to joint grants, but not so much that they prefer fully independent decision-making. Typical members donate between $250K to $20M+ per year.

- **You want to collaborate.** Funding circle members value the social rewards of giving as part of a community. They enjoy building relationships with peers, sharing knowledge, and making an impact together.

- **You already have subject-matter interest or expertise.** Funders with a deep understanding of the cause area are well-positioned to help guide the circle's strategy and grant decisions. Those who are interested in learning will gain more from a funding circle than from other ways of grantmaking. Funding circles also sometimes invite outside experts to help inform the group.

- **You have some time.** Effective participation requires a willingness to spend time reviewing applications, discussing opportunities with other members, and participating in due diligence beyond just writing checks.

Some recommended funding circles

Philanthropic advisor

What is a philanthropic advisor? Philanthropic advisors are professionals who aim to help donors maximize the impact of their charitable giving by providing strategic guidance, research, and expertise in effective giving practices.

Benefits of a philanthropic advisor:

- Strategic planning and goal-setting for charitable giving

- Due diligence on potential recipient organizations

- Impact measurement and evaluation

- Tax and legal considerations for charitable giving

- Family philanthropy coordination

- Grantmaking strategy development

- Cause area research and analysis

When to use a philanthropic advisor:

- You have mid-sized resources to donate ($100k–$5m) but limited time to research and evaluate opportunities. In many ways, hiring a philanthropic advisor is like hiring a part-time, fairly senior staff member.

- You find that you have your best conversations about philanthropy one-on-one with an expert.

- You can find a philanthropic advisor who shares your mindset, and you connect well with them interpersonally.

The field of philanthropic advisors has grown substantially in recent years, driven by increased recognition that effective philanthropy requires more than good intentions. The best modern philanthropic advisors often bring sophisticated analytical frameworks, drawing from economics, social science, and impact evaluation methodologies to help donors make evidence-based decisions.

Recommended philanthropic advisors

You'll see a few recommended advisors and networks for starters in the image below, but finding the right philanthropic advisor often means talking to a few to see who's the best fit for you.

Some recommended philanthropic advisors

Hiring grantmaking staff

What is hiring a grantmaking staff? Hiring staff is one of the clearest ways to build research and evaluation capacity toward deploying grants. Staff can dedicate serious time and focus to any cause area.

> After selling his company for a large exit, Robert has both the time and funding to establish a foundation with ambitious goals across multiple cause areas. By hiring a diverse team of experts, he created the capacity to evaluate complex opportunities while maintaining alignment with his values and vision.

Benefits of hiring a team:

- Relying on generalists who can compare across cause areas.

- Relying on specialists who can evaluate technically complex opportunities.

- Generating a stronger mission alignment than you'll typically get with external advisors.
- Fully customizing your giving to your values and priorities.

When to hire a team:

- You have lots of time. While hiring a team takes substantial upfront effort, the payoff comes later.
- You have contacts with trusted grantees who you know are ready to move to a new project. This can be a great channel for bringing on someone who already understands the space inside and out.
- You are a larger foundation planning to make large donations. For staff, plan to donate roughly $1M+ per year for one staff member, $5M+ for a team.

How to hire a team:

1. Read a book or two on vetting and hiring (e.g., *Talent* by Tyler Cowen).
2. Define the role and key responsibilities based on your foundation's needs and goals in, for example, a two- or three-page job ad.
3. Develop a rubric to consistently evaluate candidates on the traits that matter most for the role. Consider assigning weights to each trait based on its relative importance.
4. Source a diverse pool of qualified candidates through job postings, referrals, and proactive outreach.
5. Conduct resume screens to identify candidates who meet the basic requirements.
6. Run interviews focused on the key traits in your rubric. Use work samples or case studies to test for things like analytical thinking and communication skills that matter most on the job.
7. For finalists, conduct reference checks and assign a work trial project.
8. Make your hiring decision by comparing candidates based on their weighted trait scores. Trust the process, but leave room to account for intangibles too.

Remember: When bringing on a grantmaking officer, it's crucial to find someone deeply aligned with your foundation's mission and values, and who brings the analytical skills to compare grants effectively.

Do it yourself

As a retired professor, Daniel wanted full ownership of his giving decisions. He dedicated 20 hours a week to philanthropy, building deep expertise in his focus area and staying connected through grantmaker communities to avoid isolation.

What is doing it yourself? As a solo actor, you have a lot of control over your grantmaking, but it's also a lot of work. This job is a tricky one; it's hard to get feedback, and even harder to know if you're actually doing it well. Know that if you end up doing grantmaking mostly independently, it makes finding a community to connect with extra important.

Benefits of doing it yourself:

- Direct relationships with grantees.

- Being able to focus on extremely specific or niche areas.

- Ability to develop deep subject matter expertise.

- No need to worry about management or communication overhead.

- Freedom to align completely with your values.

When to do it yourself:

- You want philanthropy as your full-time commitment.

- You have a network that trusts your judgment more than external advisors would.

- You're deploying relatively modest amounts (under $200K annually).

- You can commit to developing expertise through reading, conferences, and community engagement.

How to do it yourself

The first step is becoming deeply informed. This book, including the appendix, is a great start. But now, add in at least a few more books on your cause area and on philanthropy in general (we have some recommendations at the end of this book). Try to attend some conferences and events aimed at your cause area (both donor and non-donor focused ones), and join a community with as many similar grantmakers as you can find.

Test out multiple options

Joshua initially felt torn between several approaches. He allocated small amounts to a philanthropic advisor, a funding circle, and a fund while maintaining some independent grantmaking. After a year of parallel experiments, he had clearer preferences based on experience rather than speculation.

If no single path emerges as clearly optimal, try experimenting. Most options (aside from hiring staff) can be tested at a small scale for a few months to see what works best for you.

Consider this approach when:

- Your top options score similarly in the assessment.

- You have significant uncertainty about your preferences.

- You can commit to meaningful but limited trials of multiple approaches.

- You're willing to adjust based on experience.

Overall

The question of who should be involved in making your grantmaking decisions can be less obvious than it seems at first. Many grantmakers are surprised to find out that doing it themselves might not be the best option, and to discover the wide range of options that a foundation can choose from. Many foundations will try a number of these over their lifespan, and the best cases of any approach can out-compete the average of any of the other approaches. There might not be a right answer, but there are factors that can suggest the perfect fit when it comes to deploying your grants so that they have twice as much impact.

Evaluate

Set a concrete NGO benchmark—the best option that could handle 100% of your funding.

Imagine you're a chef tasked with creating the world's greatest menu. Before you start inventing dishes, wouldn't you first want to taste what the world's best restaurants are already serving? This is the power of an evaluative benchmark, including when it comes to grantmaking.

The master craftsman's secret

A master woodworker who keeps their finest chair displayed prominently in their workshop does so not for vanity, but as a constant reminder of their quality standard. When creating something new, they compare it side-by-side with this benchmark. Is the new design truly better? Or would it be better to invest resources into reproducing what already works?

This simple practice separates professionals from amateurs. Amateurs decide what's "good enough" by gut feel. Professionals measure against concrete standards.

What makes for a good benchmark

Smart grantmakers follow the master craftsman's approach. Rather than evaluating grants in isolation, they establish clear benchmarks: proven interventions that set the bar for what "good" looks like. Every new opportunity is measured against this gold standard, asking questions like, "Is this new opportunity truly worth it, or would I have just as much or more impact by giving to my benchmark?" It's like being back at that sad restaurant with just a salad and a sandwich—except this time, you've got an amazing trail mix in your backpack. Suddenly, your options look very different.

The ideal benchmark organization meets three crucial criteria:

1. Can absorb substantial funding (ideally your entire annual budget).

2. Delivers consistent, well-understood results (with clear metrics and predictable outcomes).

3. Uses outcome frameworks/metrics comparable to your other grant opportunities (e.g., health, wealth, subjective well-being...).

With a benchmark like this, you can assess every grant against the same standard and decide whether it clears the bar, or whether you'd be better off just funding your benchmark organization. As an example, option B below serves as the benchmark because it both meets a high standard and can absorb $50M a year. Grant A is above the benchmark bar, as it is more cost-effective than B, and would therefore get funded. Grant C does not, so it is below the benchmark bar, and the grantmaker would pass on it.

Option	Cost per DALY	Room for funding	Can absorb min. spending?
A	$90	$0.1M	No
B	$100	$50M	Yes
C	$110	$1M	No
D	$120	$100M	Yes

Apply three times, and you might get lucky once

A charity executive once shared with me a maddening experience with a government official in a low-income country. One day, they'd call and need Form A. The next day, a different official would demand Form B instead. Sometimes approval came with a single phone call; other times, identical projects stalled for months.

Their solution? "Call back enough times until you get lucky."

Unfortunately, many grantmakers end up resembling these inconsistent bureaucrats more than they'd like to admit. One became so notoriously moody that applicants were told, "Only ask for money when he seems happy." But a grantmaker's mood doesn't determine a project's merit.

Without benchmarks, grantmaking falls prey to:

- **Mood distortions**: Funding decisions change based on how the grantmaker feels that day.

- **Timing luck**: Grants that arrive early in the budget cycle face different standards than those arriving later.

- **Portfolio bias**: Similar grants get rejected simply because "We just funded something like this," even if both clear the quality bar.

The moment you realize you would have funded a grant in January but rejected it in October, you know you have a consistency problem. A solid benchmark solves this. You might think that you personally are immune or only mildly affected by being tired, hungry, or having a bad day. But even judges have been found to give harsher or kinder sentences just before or after lunch. Everyone is affected by stuff like this.

The gold standard: 10 times better than cash

In development aid, a powerful benchmark has emerged: direct cash transfers to beneficiaries. Organizations like GiveDirectly simply provide money directly to people living in extreme poverty.

This creates a surprisingly high benchmark:

1. It can absorb hundreds of millions of dollars in funding.

2. Its impacts have been extensively studied across diverse contexts.

3. It provides a universal metric against which to compare other interventions that cause later increases in income.

You might think that *cash* (the affectionate short-form name for direct cash transfers as a benchmark) would be easy to beat. Shouldn't professional charities do better than just sending the money directly? Yet cash has proven remarkably hard to outperform. Major programs providing assets (like livestock), loans (like microcredit), or training (like vocational education) often deliver less value than simply giving people money directly.

Leading grantmaking organizations like GiveWell, Coefficient Giving, and even governmental aid agencies now use cash as their benchmark, often requiring potential grants to demonstrate they can deliver at least 10 times more impact per dollar than direct cash transfers. This standard remains consistent year after year, automatically filtering out weak projects.

Finding your perfect benchmark

Different causes call for different benchmarks

In education, *teaching at the right level* and *structured pedagogy* have become gold standards. These interventions improve educational quality in lower-income countries, with organizations like Pratham capable of absorbing tens of millions in funding. Many education funders explicitly compare new opportunities against these proven approaches.

For animal welfare, cage-free campaigns have emerged as a benchmark. Organizations like The Humane League (THL) convince major corporations to source eggs only from cage-free facilities, dramatically improving animal welfare at minimal cost. Animal funders increasingly measure new opportunities against THL's proven impact.

Even in fields lacking hard metrics, benchmarks remain valuable. When Charity Entrepreneurship (CE) began incubating new organizations, it used its first success, Fortify Health, as its quality benchmark. This allowed them to compare diverse projects across different cause areas, maintaining consistent standards despite different impact metrics.

Setting your bar at the right height

How do you know if your benchmark is calibrated correctly? The simplest test: if more than half of the grant opportunities you consider clear your benchmark, you've set it too low. Conversely, if you discover an exceptional organization that outperforms everything else and can absorb all your funding, perhaps that should become your new benchmark!

Being transparent about your benchmark sends a powerful signal to potential grantees. It helps organizations self-select, saving everyone time. It also communicates your standards clearly, inspiring implementing organizations to raise their game.

Snapshot summary

In our lives, we expect consistent quality and experience from the stores we shop at to the fast food we eat. Grantmakers should apply similarly consistent standards, grounded in real-world examples. A strong benchmark transforms grantmaking from a subjective art into a disciplined practice. It doesn't remove judgment, but instead gives that judgment a consistent foundation. It ensures that luck and timing don't determine which projects get funded.

The question isn't whether to have a benchmark, but which one to choose. Even a lightly held standard is significantly better than none at all.

Activity: pick a good benchmark

In order to assess grantees systematically, it can be very helpful to employ a consistent benchmark organization. This enables you to maintain high funding standards and avoid the pitfalls of arbitrary comparisons or funding without clear criteria. Today, you'll determine a benchmark against which to measure your future grants.

- Reflect on your primary cause area(s) and what success looks like in this field in terms of outcome metrics or markers.

List potential benchmark organizations or interventions in your cause area.

Benchmark idea	Funding it can absorb	How well measured it is	Comparability to other grants	Notes (details, qualifiers; etc):
	$___ M	/ 10	/ 10	
	$___ M	/ 10	/ 10	
	$___ M	/ 10	/ 10	
	$___ M	/ 10	/ 10	

Describe the top benchmark: In 2-3 sentences, explain why this benchmark is appropriate and useful for your grantmaking

Benchmark	Pros as a benchmark	Cons as a benchmark	How it will be used

Reduce

Reduce the time you take from NGOs: Aim for a maximum of two hours + one additional hour per $50K of grant.

A long rollercoaster line can ruin the ride

Imagine waiting 90 minutes for a rollercoaster that lasts only 45 seconds. As you finally stumble off the ride, you ask yourself, "Was it worth it?" That feeling of disappointment, when anticipation meets underwhelming reality, is universal. We've all experienced it, whether waiting in line for overhyped food, the latest tech gadget, or yes, that amusement park thrill ride.

Time is the one resource we can never reclaim once spent. This truth explains why excessive wait times generate such frustration. For NGOs seeking funding, every hour spent on grant applications is an hour not spent on their mission. As a grantmaker, you control this metaphorical rollercoaster line's length, clarity, and experience.

The good news is that many industries have mastered the art of managing high volumes of people efficiently. Their strategies offer valuable lessons for grant-makers.

How theme parks handle wait times (and what grantmakers can learn)

Theme parks have become masters at making necessary waits both shorter and more enjoyable. Three techniques that work for them translate directly into strong grantmaking practices:

1. **Signpost expected time investments clearly.**
   The best theme parks (and bus stops) display updated wait times prominently. Studies show this dramatically increases visitor satisfaction even when the actual wait time remains unchanged. Why? Certainty matters more than duration. Do your grantees know exactly how long your process takes? How many steps are involved? How much time does each step require? It will all help them stay cool, calm, and collected.

2. **Allow comparison to alternative options and direct people to the best one.** Smart parks display wait times for all attractions, allowing visitors to make informed choices. Maybe everyone wants to ride the newest coaster, but when they see it has a four-hour line versus 30 minutes elsewhere, they reconsider. Transparency about options empowers choice. When you clearly communicate your timelines and grant sizes, NGOs can determine if your opportunity aligns with their time budget. For bonus points, list other funders who might be better fits for certain applicants. Transparency saves everyone's time.

3. **Put eligibility requirements front and center.** The only thing worse than a long wait is reaching the front of the line just to discover you don't meet the height requirement. One grantmaker recalled his niece's afternoon of tears after waiting an hour for a ride she couldn't board. Had the requirements been clearly posted at the entrance, disappointment could have been avoided. Similarly, vague grant criteria like "We aim to improve the world" make it impossible for NGOs to self-filter, while clear criteria like "organizations under $500K annual budget led by local staff and working to improve maternal health outcomes in South Asia" make it easy.

The considerate grantmaker's formula: two hours + one hour per $50K of grant

Most grantmaking resources avoid specific time recommendations, but concrete numbers provide valuable guidance for how much time you should ideally request of potential grantees. Here's a starting point: **base application time should be no more than two hours, plus one additional hour for every $50,000 in grant amount**.

This means:

- $20K grant = 2 hours total NGO time
- $100K grant = 4 hours total NGO time
- $200K grant = 6 hours total NGO time

This only counts the NGO's time, not yours. A five-hour application form that takes you 30 minutes to review still counts as five hours. Conversely, if you read their entire annual report without requesting it specifically for your process, that's zero hours on their side.

Even these seemingly reasonable time investments multiply in real-world conditions. Consider that both parties typically explore roughly 10 opportunities for every successful match. This means those two hours for a $20K grant effectively become 20 hours of NGO time invested in fundraising rather than mission work.

The funder nobody wants to work with

Picture this: A normally punctual NGO founder arrives 10 minutes late to your meeting, disheveled and defeated. "Sorry," they explain, "I just got off a call with John."

You know John well. He has a reputation among your grantees as being extraordinarily difficult to work with, despite offering generous grants in their exact field. Many NGOs quietly warn each other away from him.

This young founder had accepted a $50K grant from John a year earlier and had already invested 80+ hours responding to his demands for documents, calls, and endless questions. They felt trapped, having already accepted his money, while his pushiness consumed their time and mental energy.

In most funding communities, there are always a few funders that NGOs warn each other about. These are typically detail-obsessed funders who value their own time highly but their grantees' time barely at all. They request information in multiple formats, prefer video responses for basic questions, or ask for specially formatted spreadsheets duplicating existing budgets.

A revealing comparison of John's process for a $100K grant shows the imbalance:

Steps in John's process for a 100k grant	Time cost for John	Time cost for NGO
First application process	0.5 hours	3 hours
Initial interview	1 hour	2 hours
Email back and forth	2 hours	8 hours
Deeper application	2 hours	20 hours
Ongoing conversations	5 hours	10 hours

The funder NGOs love

Sarah, another detail-oriented funder, consistently receives praise from the same NGOs that dread John's emails. "They know so much about our work and ask insightful questions," grantees say. What makes the difference?

Sarah respects NGO time as much as her own. She dives deep into research, attends conferences, and studies the field extensively, all on her own time. Rather than peppering grantees with every question that crosses her mind, she researches answers herself and has focused conversations twice yearly. Her calls are well-prepared, substantive, and end exactly on schedule.

Sarah also coordinates with other funders, sharing applications and assessments when possible to prevent NGOs from answering identical questions repeatedly. She regularly reevaluates her process: How long does it take grantees? How many apply for each grant awarded? Is her website clear about who might be a good fit?

Her process for a $100K grant looks strikingly different:

Steps in Sarah's process for a $100K grant	Time cost for Sarah	Time cost for NGO
Deep dive into the cause area	10 hours	0 hours
First application process	0.1 hours	2 hours
Initial interview	2 hours	2 hours
Deeper application	5 hours	3 hours

Though Sarah's process requires a greater time investment on her part than John's, she places the burden on herself rather than the NGO. This approach recognizes that grantmaking is a partnership, not a dictatorship. Funders bring financial resources; NGOs bring talent and implementation expertise. Neither succeeds without the other.

GiveWell's public grant process is another great example of being clear and respectful of NGO time, but on a larger and more institutional level.

Going deeper: practical applications

Be transparent about your target audience

One common mistake is vague criteria that leave NGOs guessing. Imagine a job posting that said "Looking for human, ideally earth-based." It would attract irrelevant applications while serious candidates would scroll past. When your criteria lack specificity, the strongest NGOs often assume they don't qualify. Even if you're still exploring, provide examples of past grants or areas you definitely won't fund.

Optimize your first screening step

Think of your initial application as a movie trailer—just enough to determine interest. This first step should give you sufficient information to decide if the full "movie" (more than two hours of engagement) is worthwhile. Beyond basics like contact information and a brief project description (under 250 words), ask just three questions, each answerable in three sentences. Well-chosen questions can effectively filter hundreds of applications down to dozens, ruling out 90% of grants.

Here's an example of the three questions:

1. What goals are you setting for yourself for the grant you are applying for? (one to three goals/SMART goals)

2. Briefly give us a sense of why you think this grant is important/one of the more cost-effective options for us to consider? (around three to five sentences)

3. Pre-mortem: Imagine it's two years from now, and your project has failed to achieve its intended impact. What were the biggest reasons for this failure, and how could they have been prevented? (around three to five sentences each)

Beware the "mercenary NGO" trap

The power imbalance between funders and NGOs sometimes leads to foundations funding organizations that will do anything for money rather than those truly aligned with the foundation's mission. Unlike for-profit contractors providing specific services, NGO grants require higher trust and typically involve fewer measurable outcomes. Look for partners who share your vision instead of merely following your instructions because you're paying.

Question the value of "extra services"

Some foundations offer mentorship, consulting, or training alongside funding. While these can add value, they often don't. Ask yourself: "Would NGOs pay for this service if offered by a non-funder? Would they attend it for free if it were offered by someone else?" If not, they're likely participating to secure funding rather than because they find it inherently valuable.

A partnership perspective

Having a framework for appropriate time investment is challenging, but two hours plus one hour per $50,000 granted provides a useful guideline. Design application processes that start concisely and gradually deepen with fewer applicants. When you thoughtfully consider NGO time spent alongside your own needs, you'll find organizations enjoy working with you, and your grantee relationships improve over time.

NGOs bring the talent, and grantmakers bring the funding. If both sides align on what they want to accomplish (and are thoughtful about the time and effort they ask of each other) then treating it as a true partnership can unlock a huge amount of impact.

Activity: the time cost of your application process

For each step below, map out a possible plan, along with how much time it would take you (the funder) to evaluate it and how much time it would take the NGO to complete.

Step 1: How did you hear about the grant?

This doesn't count toward your time estimate, since the NGO has already done it. But it's still worth considering. If you only hear about NGOs that were already selected by another grantmaker, they've already invested time in that earlier process.

	NGO time cost:	Funder time cost:

Step 2: Set your pre-application phase

What information do you plan to give the grantee before they apply?
What can you say to narrow down the field?

	NGO time cost:	Funder time cost:

Step 3: What does your first application step look like?

This would be your top three questions, as well as the basic information you are asking for.

	NGO time cost:	Funder time cost:

Step 4: What does your deeper dive look like?

What steps would you take for a deeper investigation? Examples of this might be an interview call (one hour per 30 minutes of interview) or a deeper writeup (around two hours per novel page of writing).

	NGO time cost:	Funder time cost:

Total time cost for the NGO:

Total time cost for the funder:

Average size of grant:

Substance

Focus on substance over style, and know how the charity works.

Don't be fooled by glitter (or, why the worst charity got the most money)

The auditorium fell silent as the first presenter took the stage. This was philanthropy's version of *Shark Tank*—eight pitches for new charities, with a networking wine break at intermission. In the audience, nervous founders clutched notes while funders like me reviewed the brief fact sheets in our laps.

The first speaker was magnetic, weaving emotional stories with impressive data points, her slides crisp and colorful. When she mentioned a child whose life had been transformed by their health-worker training program, I noticed someone nearby dabbing away tears. She exited to thunderous applause.

Then came the second presenter, a stark contrast. His glasses were thicker than his stack of notes, his clothes a size too large, and he stumbled through every third word. His slides? Black-and-white text bombs with citations in microscopic font. Around me, people checked their phones or stifled yawns. His presentation ended with scattered, pitiful applause. Both charities worked in the same field: training health workers in low- and middle-income countries.

Unlike the judges on *Shark Tank*, I didn't need to make an immediate decision. At home, I put on my own slightly-too-big glasses and began digging into the data. What I discovered was illuminating: The polished presenter's charity was objectively worse. Despite her glossy materials, she spent extravagantly to deliver nearly identical training at five times the cost of the awkward presenter's organization. The charity's outcomes fell below industry benchmarks for effectiveness and sustainability, while the "boring" charity was outperforming on virtually every impact metric.

Yet one thrived while the other struggled. The stylish charity had doubled its budget annually since inception—not because it delivered better results, but because it told a better story. It had mastered the art of communication, but failed at cost-effective impact.

This pattern repeats across philanthropy: organizations grow based on communication skills (writing, websites, public speaking) regardless of their underlying effectiveness. Communication skills are valuable, but they're not what we're "buying" in the charity world. If an organization delivers exceptional results, should we really care whether its PowerPoint slides sparkle?

What is style vs. substance?

To distinguish between style and substance, consider these contrasting elements:

Style	Substance
• Public speaking skills	• A good price tag
• Sharp website and marketing	• Data-driven and honest website
• Strong branding/name recognition	• A strong evidence base
• A clean and graphic newsletter	• Clear theory of change
• Good video or podcast appearances	• Beating industry benchmarks
• Public media attention	• External reviews
• Celebrity endorsements (e.g., athletes, musicians)	• Expert endorsements (e.g., grantmakers, academics in the field)
• A team that looks good	• A team that executes well

While some exceptional charities excel in both categories, these qualities often conflict. The most stylish website makes bold impact claims and leads with emotional stories, directly contradicting the cautious approach of evidence-based work. The polished charity I observed made grander claims about its impact, but these claims collapsed under scrutiny. Honesty is frequently penalized in marketing materials.

The case of the life-saving bus

Consider this common fundraising claim: "Save a life for $10!" accompanied by a child's image on a bus advertisement. It's compelling, especially considering GiveWell's top charities save lives for a pricey $3,500 each.

The real difference lies in the rigor of measurement. The bus charity claims to provide life-saving bednets for $10 each. While a bednet *could* save a life, in reality, many need to be distributed to save one. By contrast, GiveWell's Against Malaria Foundation distributes nets for about $3 each. This makes the bus charity less than half as effective (not to mention misleading) about its impact.

Beyond impressive claims: lessons from the youngest peer-reviewed author

The youngest person to publish in a peer-reviewed medical journal demonstrated the power of substance over style. At the age of 9, Emily Rosa designed an elegantly simple experiment to test "therapeutic touch" practitioners who claimed to manipulate human energy fields:

1. She sat practitioners at a table with a divider.

2. They placed their hands through holes in the divider.

3. Emily held her hand above one of their hands at random.

4. Practitioners had to identify which hand sensed her "energy field."

Despite their confident claims, practitioners were correct only 44% of the time in 280 trials—that's worse than random chance. This simple experiment demolished pseudoscientific claims through methodological rigor.

The NGO world contains many similarly misleading claims. Like Emily, funders need to put ideas to the test rather than accepting emotional stories or plausible theories. While medicine has established evidence standards, charity evaluation remains inconsistent. But the same rule of evidence and science applies to both.

Evidence-based practice pyramid showing the strongest methods at the top

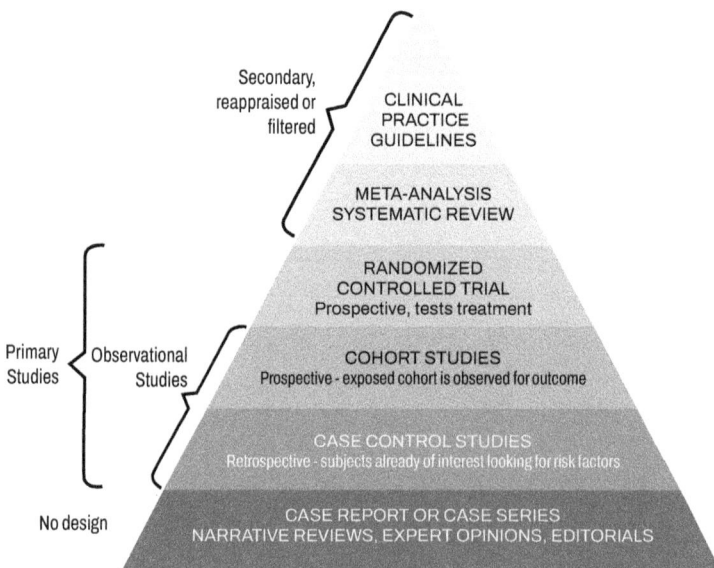

A great charity's staff will not just be doing something because they think it works or because they have an emotional story suggesting it works (that type of evidence is right at the bottom of the pyramid). Instead, they will provide robust studies demonstrating effectiveness, ideally with multiple supporting studies across different contexts. This evidence, combined with cost data, shows funders exactly what outcomes they're purchasing.

A table that can predict the future: The theory of change

(No, this one does not pass the evidence test.)

Beyond evidence for whether an intervention works in general, funders need to understand how specific organizational actions connect to desired outcomes. This requires a clear theory of change: a roadmap showing how inputs (like immunization camps and financial incentives) lead to intermediate outcomes (increased immunization rates) and ultimately to goals (reduced child mortality). We don't care about the camps; we care about the lives saved. The best way to see this is using a theory-of-change document.

Theory of change for new incentives

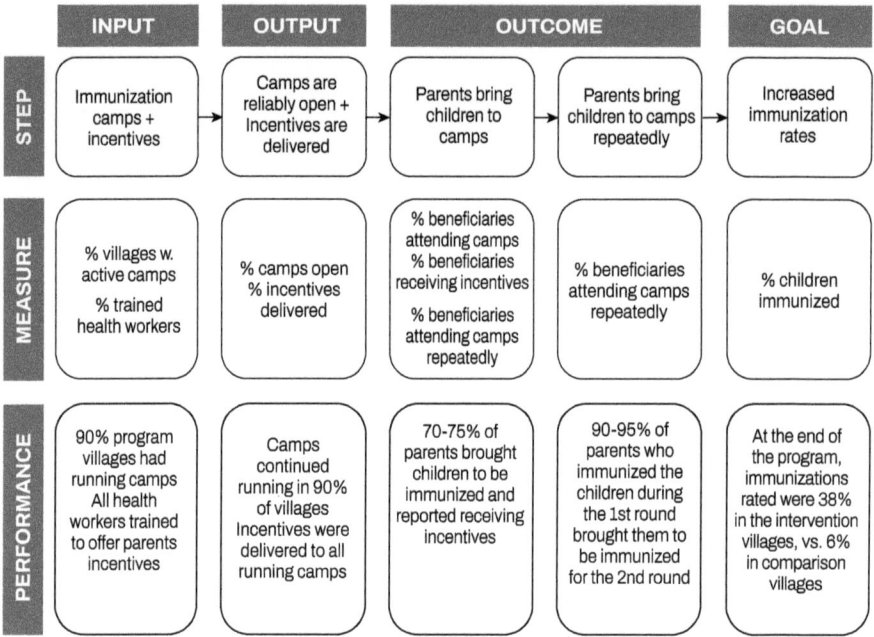

	INPUT	OUTPUT	OUTCOME		GOAL
STEP	Immunization camps + incentives	Camps are reliably open + Incentives are delivered	Parents bring children to camps	Parents bring children to camps repeatedly	Increased immunization rates
MEASURE	% villages w. active camps % trained health workers	% camps open % incentives delivered	% beneficiaries attending camps % beneficiaries receiving incentives % beneficiaries attending camps repeatedly	% beneficiaries attending camps repeatedly	% children immunized
PERFORMANCE	90% program villages had running camps All health workers trained to offer parents incentives	Camps continued running in 90% of villages Incentives were delivered to all running camps	70-75% of parents brought children to be immunized and reported receiving incentives	90-95% of parents who immunized the children during the 1st round brought them to be immunized for the 2nd round	At the end of the program, immunizations rated were 38% in the intervention villages, vs. 6% in comparison villages

These tables can show you what actions the charity is taking and how they lead to the next step. They can also highlight which steps are most uncertain and establish measurement points to diagnose problems if outcomes don't materialize. Unlike an Ouija board, a good theory of change doesn't just make predictions; it explains causal mechanisms clearly enough to be testable.

The board that looks great but ties charities' shoelaces together

Many NGOs prioritize style over substance in their governance structures. A truly effective board focuses on:

- Financial oversight and accountability

- Executive hiring, evaluation, and compensation

- Strategic guidance and risk management

Yet most funders (and consequently, NGOs) emphasize style elements:

- Impressive résumés and famous names who rarely contribute meaningfully

- Visual diversity without substantive diversity of perspectives or relevant experience

- Excessively large boards (eight to 12 members) that look impressive but function poorly compared to smaller, more engaged boards (three to five members)

When evaluating an organization, three highly involved board members contribute more than 12 impressive names and credentials. Ask how many hours each board member invests (NGOs usually answer honestly), but recognize that board composition matters far less than the implementing team, which often receives less website attention.

The best charity I donated to had no website

Some truly exceptional organizations lack style entirely. I once discovered a university-based initiative with only a text-heavy departmental webpage filled with hyperlinked citations. Even their name was difficult to pronounce (Schistosomiasis Control Initiative).

But their evidence was extraordinary, with rigorous studies showing that treating intestinal worms for $0.50 per child dramatically increased school attendance. Speaking with the founder revealed a humble, pragmatic academic who deeply understood his program's mechanics and potential failure points.

This experience was perspective-changing: What if the most effective charities lack glossy marketing? What if they seem plain or even boring? It felt like discovering there's no Santa Claus—a disillusionment that revealed how unfair our system of charitable support truly is.

Going deeper: testing for substance

What does a good evidence base look like? One useful way to present evidence is in a simple evidence table. For example, the one below looks at different ways to reduce stress and shows how much evidence exists for each approach.

Intervention	Strength of Effect	Studies Reviewed	Quality of Evidence	Notes
8-week CBT programme	54%	86 studies	High	53% reduction in salivary cortisol; 55.53% reduction in anxiety sensitivity. Studies showed statistically significant results (2/2, 100%).
Single sessions mindfulness meditation (10-20 mins)	7%	11 studies	High	13% reduction in stress scores; 5.88% decrease in STAI score. Studies showed statistically significant results (3/3, 100%)
Yoga (Sudarshan Kriya)	27%	2 studies	High	35.17% decrease in general distress anxiety score; 19.13% decrease in blood cortisol. Studies showed statistically significant results (2/2, 100%)
10 mins listening to music (Classical or personal)	16%	24 studies	Medium	1.98% decrease in salivary cortisol; 29.40% additional decrease in systolic blood pressure. Studies showed statistically significant results (2/3).
25-50g of dark chocolate daily	21%	2 studies	Low	7.47% decrease in blood cortisol; 35.2% decrease in salivary cortisol. Studies showed statistically significant Results (2/2, 100%)

The transcript test: separating charisma from content

Ever been mesmerized by a speaker only to later wonder what exactly they said? Here's a simple mental exercise I use to detect substance beneath style: imagine reading a transcript of the talk instead of watching the performance. When you strip away the confident gestures, dramatic pauses, and winning smile, do those "profound insights" suddenly seem shallow or obvious? That's a red flag that style, not substance, was doing the heavy lifting. However, if the ideas remain compelling, well-reasoned, and evidence-based even on paper, you've likely found someone with genuine expertise. This "transcript test" works remarkably well for charity pitches, TED talks, and even political speeches. It helps you invest your attention (and donations) where they'll truly make a difference rather than simply feeling good in the moment.

Bottom line: choose substance

The most impactful giving decisions prioritize operational excellence and evidence over presentation polish. When substance drives your giving, your dollars accomplish more good in the world.

What seemingly "boring" charity might be hiding an extraordinary impact behind an unpolished exterior? And how might your giving change if evidence, rather than emotion, guided every donation?

Activity: a two-page grant review that has substance

Overall summary									
Description of project:									
Idea			**Team**			**Execution**			**Other**
Cost effectiveness	Evidence based	Neglect	Values	Science minded	Ability	Understanding of space	Growth mindset	Track record	Red flags
/10	/10	/10	/10	/10	/10	/10	/10	/10	/10

Key factors/Cruxes	
Biggest non-crux strength of the project	**Biggest non-crux weakness of the project**
Conclusion and overall score	

Steps to conduct + full link	Summary description
First application	
First interview	

Follow-up questions that could be good to ask	
Other supporting documents	

Idea

Criteria	Cost effectiveness	Evidence based	Neglect	Red/green flags
Score	X/10	X/10	X/10	X/10
Explanation				

Team

Criteria	Values	Science minded	Competence	Red/green flags
Score	X/10	X/10	X/10	X/10
Explanation				

Execution

Criteria	Understanding of space	Self-awareness / Open-mindedness	Track record	Red/green flags
Score	X/10	X/10	X/10	X/10
Explanation				

Link to spreadsheet WFM (template): [24]	
Link to benchmark organization scorecard:	

The POWERS in a nutshell

There are some common and cross-applicable methods that can help grant-makers create more impact with their grants, regardless of scope.

• **P**rice tag: *Good grantmakers should know the price tag (and how much impact it buys) for every grant they give.*

• **O**ptions: *Good grantmakers compare 10 or more options for every grant they give.*

• **W**ho: *Good grantmakers do not always decide on their own grants.*

• **E**valuate: *Good grantmakers set a concrete NGO benchmark. This is the best option that could handle 100% of their funding.*

• **R**educe: *Good grantmakers reduce the time they take from NGOs, aiming for a maximum of two hours + one additional hour per $50k of grant.*

• **S**ubstance: *Good grantmakers focus on substance over style and know how the charity works.*

It can be hard to be a good grantmaker and keep all the principles in mind, but with a narrow scope and good strategic planning, it can massively increase each grant's impact.

CHAPTER 3

Building Your Grantmaking Community

If you want to go fast, go alone; if you want to go far, go together.

The solo funder's dilemma: fast vs. far

I know two funders who work in the same space. Both were thoughtful and intelligent, but with one big difference: one was isolated while the other was deeply connected to the rest of the grantmaking community. The first funder's isolation was not entirely by choice; she was in a challenging time zone, for example, and could not travel much due to a family member with a medical condition. Regardless of the reasons, the difference in outcomes between the two funders was stark. The connected funder tended to see more opportunities, hear about new ideas first, and was able to get the consistent motivational conversations that the isolated funder lacked. Over time, this interconnected knowledge built up and enabled the connected funder to make better and better grants, and to influence others to do so, too.

It might sometimes feel quicker just to focus on your own work and get more grants out the door, but being connected to a community is worth its weight in gold. There are foundations that take this too far, spending most of their time talking to other funders, but a decent rule of thumb is this: if you're spending less than 5% of your time speaking to other funders in the ecosystem, you are probably missing out. In the short term, your knowledge will be limited, and in the long term, your philanthropic motivation will also be at risk.

The ancient proverb holds here: **If you want to go fast, go alone; if you want to go far, go together.**

What's more, books and frameworks can only take you so far. The most successful philanthropists recognize that their greatest impact comes from community connections that expand their vision beyond their own perspective. In the remainder of this book, we'll explore two key sources of community.

Community source No. 1: your personal network

Your network is likely the first place you will start sharing and building ideas. Your existing relationships (family members, foundation colleagues, professional contacts) represent a hugely promising community. These connections can be sounding boards, but they can also help multiply your impact.

For most grantmakers, their network holds 10 times more power than their individual resources. Becoming a trusted leader in that network could mean 10 times the funding directed toward the causes you care about most.

Your biggest philanthropic impact might not come from your direct grantmaking but instead from connecting others to key ideas, organizations, and principles.

Unlocking this network effect doesn't happen through argumentative conversion attempts. Instead, it requires patience, thoughtful communication, and recognition that people adopt new ideas at different rates:

- **Innovators** (that's likely you, since you're reading about improving your grantmaking) eagerly explore new approaches.

- **Early adopters** quickly embrace well-explained innovations.

- **The majority** need more evidence and peer examples.

- **Laggards** may remain skeptical indefinitely.

When sharing ideas with those in your network, half the battle is won by picking the right people. Who might be a good partner in your journey? Who is most likely to co-fund a great grant with you?

Community source No. 2: external communities

While your personal network amplifies your impact, specialized philanthropic communities accelerate your learning. These peer groups (formal giving circles, foundation networks, online communities, or informal gatherings) connect you with a community of like-minded people.

Imagine having access to a brain trust of experienced funders who can help you do the following:

- Evaluate new approaches before committing resources.

- Identify oversights in your giving strategy.

- Discover organizations doing groundbreaking work.

- Share due diligence to reduce redundant effort.

- Navigate complex challenges with the benefit of others' experiences.

Everyone is deeply affected by their closest peers. Surround yourself with thoughtful, effective grantmakers, and your own giving will naturally evolve toward greater impact.

Research consistently shows that grantmakers who actively participate in philanthropic communities give more, give more effectively, and report greater satisfaction with their giving. This makes joining a community perhaps the single most important step you can take to advance your grantmaking journey.

Breaking the isolation barrier

Many new funders hesitate to join philanthropic communities, worried about appearing inexperienced or being judged for their wealth. This reluctance is natural but ultimately limiting. Most established giving communities enthusiastically welcome new members and go out of their way to create supportive, learning-oriented environments.

If you're already part of a community but find it's not meeting all your needs, consider joining another. Different communities offer different perspectives, and your participation in multiple groups creates valuable cross-pollination of ideas.

The best grantmakers are connectors. They bring good ideas from one community into another, forge relationships across traditional boundaries, and create networks that strengthen the philanthropic ecosystem.

Amplifying

Your network is typically 10 times more powerful than you are as an individual.

Amplification: a cross-cutting tool

Maya stumbled across a remarkable nonprofit that had developed a water filtration system, preventing deadly diseases at just $2 per person, a fraction of typical costs. Impressed by the evidence and cost-effectiveness, she donated $10,000, protecting 5,000 lives and making a meaningful difference.

But instead of stopping there, Maya shared this discovery with strategic connections: her colleague who ran a family foundation, a former university classmate who recently had a successful business exit, and her monthly investment group. Within weeks, her initial discovery triggered commitments totaling $150,000. When one impressed investor introduced the nonprofit to her company's corporate giving program, that amount grew to $400,000.

Maya's original $10,000 donation was multiplied 40-fold without requiring additional funds from her, simply through thoughtful sharing with the right people at the right time. This is the power of amplification: transforming individual impact into something exponentially greater through a network's collective resources.

Early in our giving journeys, most of us recognize the potential of working with others. Amplification occurs when your grant catalyzes additional funding that exceeds your initial contribution. It's an exciting prospect: influencing just one person who donates similarly to you can instantly double your impact!

However, this approach requires finesse if you want to avoid becoming the person everyone steers clear of at dinner parties, the one bombarding friends with charity statistics or graphic descriptions of suffering. Here's how to share your philanthropic passion without alienating your network.

The listener's advantage

Listen before you speak. When we're passionate about a cause, our natural instinct is to broadcast that enthusiasm. But effective persuasion begins with understanding the person across from you.

Consider James, who spent years unsuccessfully trying to convince his wealthy uncle to fund global health initiatives. James would always pitch his uncle on how cost-effective the initiatives were. During a holiday gathering, James finally asked why his uncle seemed resistant. The answer surprised him: "I built my business in this community. I feel responsible to give back here." With this insight, James shifted his approach, introducing his uncle to a cost-effective mental health organization that had launched a pilot program in their city. Within a year, his uncle became one of the program's largest supporters.

Before sharing your philanthropic insights, discover:

- What motivates others to give (or not give)
- A person's existing knowledge about philanthropy
- Whose opinions the person respects
- The person's values and priorities

This listening-first approach demonstrates humility while helping you determine if your philanthropic path might align with theirs.

The door-to-door strategy: finding your natural allies

Focus energy on the naturally curious

A friend once won a door-to-door sales competition using a simple strategy: "I went to the door, and if they weren't keen, I just moved on to the next door right away without fuss."

This wisdom applies perfectly to philanthropic influence. For some folks, effective giving principles instantly "click," and the person feels they now have answers to questions they didn't know how to ask. These individuals are your natural allies and the most receptive audience.

Start with the already engaged

When Lauren, a tech executive, discovered effective altruism, she didn't broadcast it to her entire network. Instead, she identified five colleagues who regularly discussed social impact over lunch. She shared a compelling book with them, sparking conversations that eventually led three of them to redirect substantial portions of their giving to more effective charities.

Your intuition can help identify these receptive individuals. Starting with the similarly minded creates momentum and builds a coalition that can help influence others.

Speaking their language: the translation effect

When Maria wanted to encourage her animal-loving sister to support more effective charities, she didn't lecture about cost-effectiveness or global priorities. Instead, she shared how factory farming interventions could prevent suffering for millions of animals at a scale that local shelters couldn't match. By connecting to her sister's existing passion rather than trying to replace it, Maria helped expand her giving without diminishing her commitment to animal welfare.

This tailored approach may seem obvious, but it's surprisingly easy to forget amid our enthusiasm. Effective amplification isn't about making a universal case for effective giving. It's about making a personalized case that respects and builds upon each individual's values.

Adapt your message to existing values

The same cause can be framed in dramatically different ways that resonate with different audiences.

All in the family: navigating your closest network

Working with family on giving can be powerful, albeit tricky. Some families use a formal vehicle, such as a family foundation or a donor-advised fund (money set aside for grants). Others coordinate more informally. Either way, clear roles and strong communication can increase the impact of family dynamics.

Consider these approaches for effective family engagement:

1. Show up consistently

Jason, a recent college graduate, volunteered to take notes during his family's foundation meetings. This small commitment grew over three years into leadership of a major grantmaking initiative after he demonstrated consistent interest and developed expertise that his family valued.

Simply expressing a genuine, sustained interest in your family's philanthropy can gradually increase your influence. Many families struggle to engage younger generations, but your enthusiasm can fill this gap.

2. Celebrate progress, not perfection

One family made its first grant to a promising but unproven intervention. Though the grant was tiny compared to their usual giving, their daughter, who had always championed the change, celebrated as though they'd won an Olympic medal. Her positive reinforcement led to increasingly substantial and strategic grants in subsequent years.

Change happens incrementally, especially within families. When a family makes even a small step toward more effective giving, enthusiastic recognition often accomplishes more than critiquing its limitations.

3. Time it right and keep it light

Knowing that her family became combative around holidays, Rebecca instead brought up new giving ideas during summer gatherings when everyone was more relaxed. She also tied these conversations to shared family interests, gradually introducing effective giving principles without always labeling them as directly related to philanthropy.

If philanthropy discussions consistently create tension, you're likely pushing too hard. Connect giving conversations to natural opportunities and existing interests.

4. Become the family expert

After his grandfather expressed interest in mental health initiatives, Michael immersed himself in the research, taking online courses and speaking with experts. When the family later decided to fund mental health programs, they naturally turned to him for guidance on the most effective approaches.

Deep knowledge of a cause area that resonates with your family can make you an invaluable resource. This position allows you to guide decisions based on evidence, even if you're the only one researching effectiveness.

5. Be a connector, not a barrier

Despite her expertise in global education, Sophia's family still saw her as "the impulsive one," dismissing her funding recommendations. Rather than repeatedly hitting this wall, Sophia invited Dr. Reyes, a respected education researcher, to present at their foundation's quarterly meeting. While her family had ignored Sophia's identical points about evidence-based literacy programs, they were captivated by Dr. Reyes's presentation and approved a significant grant that day. Sophia realized her most valuable role wasn't as the expert herself but as the bridge between her family and the external voices they would trust.

Some people may never be seen as the family expert. If you are always "the baby" no matter how many degrees you hold, becoming a family expert may not be your best bet. At the end of the day, though, you don't need to be the one to convince your family. You can connect them to the person who is more likely to resonate with them.

If you know another funder who might connect better with an older family member than you would, introduce them. Maybe your brother would never listen to you, but he would take a call with a brilliant nonprofit leader you know. Don't be a barrier between your family and others advocating for the same areas you are; instead, be a connector.

Boardroom dynamics: amplifying through governance

A vital component of impactful philanthropy is the relationship between grant-makers and their boards. Depending on your role within the foundation or philanthropic entity, your relationship with the board can vary significantly. For instance, the dynamics between you and board members will differ substantially if you are a family member, a foundation employee, or working with external advisors or partners. These relationships play a significant role in guiding the strategic direction and governance of your foundation. In short, a strong, collaborative relationship with your board is indispensable if high-impact philanthropy is your goal.

Still, conflicts and tensions between grantmakers and their boards are often inevitable. They can stem from a wide range of sources: differing visions for the organization's future, strategic priorities, or views on how to evaluate success and impact. For instance, one grantmaker might be passionate about riskier global health projects, while the more cautious board members may insist on the most conservative projects. Similarly, rigorous, data-driven evaluation methods might be off-putting to a board more accustomed to qualitative assessments. Any number of differences such as these are possible. What's important is that you recognize and navigate them without letting them derail your efforts.

1. Establish clear communication rhythms

When Lisa joined a family foundation as a program officer, she implemented monthly dashboard reports highlighting both successes and challenges. This regular communication gave board members confidence to approve her more ambitious proposals during quarterly meetings. A fixed schedule typically works better than impromptu meetings.

Regular, transparent updates build trust and prevent surprises.

2. Tap into the brain trust

Marco created specialized committees that played to each board member's strengths instead of expecting everyone to contribute equally to all decisions. When considering a major global health initiative, he asked Dr. Shapiro to chair a small review team while separately engaging the foundation's finance expert on funding models. This targeted approach not only produced stronger recommendations but dramatically increased board engagement. Members who had previously seemed disinterested now actively contributed in their areas of expertise.

Board members are often a goldmine of knowledge and experience, and utilizing their diverse expertise can significantly amplify your impact. This can involve creating committees within the board to address specific areas, such as M&E (monitoring and evaluation), strategy, or stakeholder engagement. Be careful with their time, though, as it's often in short supply.

3. Foster a culture of learning

Amara introduced a five-minute "learning spotlight" at each board meeting, sharing success stories from peer foundations and gradually introducing impact evaluation frameworks. Board members soon began requesting these segments and even volunteering to present their own findings from philanthropy research. When the foundation later faced a funding shortfall, members applied their new evaluative thinking to make difficult but more strategic decisions rather than simply cutting grants across the board.

Cultivating a culture of continuous learning and growth among board members and staff is essential for the foundation's ability to adapt and increase its impact. This could mean analyzing case studies of similar philanthropic efforts, holding regular discussions on emerging trends in philanthropy, assessing the outcomes of past grantmaking efforts, or reviewing feedback from grantees and other stakeholders. To accomplish this, you will likely need to model this behavior rather than wait for board members to do so.

4. Make being a good board member easy

Carlos replaced his information-heavy presentations with one-page executive summaries featuring clear bullet points and single-sentence proposals. He also prepared color-coded decision trees showing exactly how each grant aligned with their strategic priorities. Board members who normally deferred decisions to follow-up meetings began making immediate and favorable decisions, with one long-serving member admitting, "This is the first time I've truly understood what we're voting on."

The more distilled your information, the better (think: executive summaries and single-sentence explanations). When time is tight, board members tend to think less critically and default to familiar habits. If you want them to seriously consider a new idea, you'll need to disrupt that pattern. The best way to do that is by boiling things down to the most essential considerations.

If you embed these principles early and consistently in your relationship with the board, you'll be better positioned to avoid the pitfalls that can derail both board dynamics and, ultimately, your impact.

Beyond your circle: influencing the wider philanthropic world

Your journey to impact does not end with your personal network. While you may already be connected to people with wealth to donate and an appetite for impact, the wider philanthropic world holds an even greater number of opportunities to promote effective giving. No matter how large your network is, there are more resources outside it than within it. After all, philanthropists and individual donors in the U.S. alone give hundreds of billions of dollars a year. Consider this a flashing neon invitation for you to influence such large-scale giving for the better.

While mainstream philanthropy has done an incredible amount of good for the world, there is still a lot of uncertainty about how to define and pursue "effective" giving. Philanthropic networks and organizations provide spaces to have these kinds of conversations. By engaging with these groups, you'll find like-minded individuals open to evolving their giving practices, and likely able to improve yours as well by broadening your understanding of the philanthropic landscape.

Creating amplification by sharing grants

The impact of your grants can echo throughout the philanthropic world, influencing people you've never even met. For example, let's say you make a strategic donation to a promising but overlooked initiative. This could stop with you, but you could also forward the reasons you made the grant to three other funders you know. Taking it a step further, you could write up a public post on why you support this grant vs. others.

Of course, your signal is only as strong as your reputation. Even so, funders' words can carry outsized weight. A mention from GiveWell, or public praise for a grantee's approach, for example, can redirect serious money. Endorsements from respected decision-makers like authors, professors, and field experts can have a similar effect. You can build comparable credibility by becoming a specialist in a clear niche. Remember to always share your process and grant decisions because transparency grows the field's knowledge. It also sets a norm others can follow.

The power of matching campaigns

Matching campaigns are a popular and dynamic tool for multiplying the impact of individual donations. By promising to match donations to a selected recipient within a set period, these campaigns can effectively double or triple the value of each contribution. Their broad appeal is understandable: simply advertising your own commitment to donate can result in a massive increase in overall donations. A study by the Abdul Latif Jameel Poverty Action Lab (J-PAL) found that merely announcing that matching funds are available increased charities' revenue per solicitation by 19%.

The collaboration imperative

Lasting impact ultimately stems from thoughtful collaboration within your network, across foundations, and with government and civil society partners. The most successful philanthropists balance internal strategy development with external relationship building, recognizing that their greatest contributions often emerge from the connections they forge between people, ideas, and resources.

As you develop your amplification approach, remember that this work requires both patience and flexibility. Sometimes you'll focus on refining your own giving strategy; other times you'll prioritize building partnerships. This natural oscillation between reflection and connection strengthens both your individual giving and your influence within the broader philanthropic community.

Connect

You are the sum of your five closest peers. Surround yourself with great grantmakers, and you'll make better grants.

The importance of connection

In my experience, grantmakers who connect with each other are often happier and make more effective grants. Grantmaking can be socially isolating, and often, there are conversations that flow most naturally with others who are making substantial donations. We've found that the most impactful grantmakers typically have a community they rely on for ideas, advice, and shared opportunities. One of the most valuable takeaways from this book is understanding the importance of (and finding pathways into) a supportive community.

Who to connect with?

Below is a quick quiz to help you identify communities worth exploring first. These recommendations are intended as starting points rather than definitive matches. To truly understand a community, you'll typically need to read about it, explore its website, and ideally have direct interaction with members. Thankfully, there are many communities beyond those listed here; we've included only those that the coauthors or their close contacts have personal experience with. We also encourage you to join and explore multiple communities.

Quick community fit quiz!

- What do you want your community to be focused on?
    - **Events**: Regular conferences and gatherings where philanthropists connect in person.
    - **Giving**: Structured approaches to donating, often with pledges or collective funding.
    - **Network**: Ongoing peer relationships and information-sharing between funders.
    - **Learning:** Skill-building and knowledge-acquisition through structured programs.
- Do you want your community to be based around a cause area?
    - No, not that important
    - Yes, based around human health and development.
    - Yes, based around animal welfare/the environment.
    - Yes, based around another cause area, such as social justice.

Based on your answers, take a look at the following table of some recommended communities.

	No specific cause area	Humans / global health	Animals / environment	Other (e.g., social justice)
Event focused	TED Nexus Global	Skoll OC Global	AVA The Conduit	Edge Funders HRFN
Giving focused	GWWC Founders Pledge Giving Pledge	LYCS Global Health Funding Circle	Strategic Animal Funding Circle Resource justice	Generation Pledge Bolder Giving

Network focused	Effective Altruism	Big Bang Philanthropy	Senterra Funders	Resource Generation
	P150	Kokoro	Environmental Funders Network	Ariadne Network
Learning focused	AIM: Grantmaking Program Forward Global			

No specific cause area

Events focused

TED (Technology, Entertainment, Design) (ted.com)

The nonprofit organization devoted to spreading ideas, usually through short, powerful talks (18 minutes or less), was founded in 1984 as a conference where "technology, entertainment, and design" converged. TED now covers almost all topics, from science to business, in more than 100 languages. TED is a global community that welcomes people from every discipline and culture who seek a deeper understanding of the world. The organization believes passionately in the power of ideas to change ideas, transform lives, and ultimately, shape the world. It has a large philanthropy community mixed with other members and runs an active multi-funder initiative called the Audacious Project.

Nexus Global (nexusglobal.org)

This is an international network of individuals, organizations, and businesses dedicated to advancing social entrepreneurship, NGOs, and impact investing. It brings together diverse stakeholders (entrepreneurs, investors, philanthropists, and policymakers) who share a common goal of using market-based solutions to address social and environmental challenges. Nexus Global hosts events and workshops to facilitate collaboration and knowledge-sharing among its members.

Giving focused

Giving What We Can (GWWC) (givingwhatwecan.org)

An effective giving organization, GWWC encourages individuals to pledge a portion of their income (typically 10%) to highly effective charities. Members believe that by donating to rigorously evaluated charities focused on impact and cost-effectiveness, they can maximize the good accomplished through charitable giving. GWWC provides resources and support to help members make informed decisions and conducts research to identify the most effective charities and interventions.

Founders Pledge (founderspledge.com)

This community of entrepreneurs and startup founders is made up of those who have pledged to donate a portion of their personal proceeds from their company's exit (through acquisition or IPO) to charity. Members believe successful entrepreneurs have a unique opportunity and responsibility to create a positive impact with their wealth. By pledging exit proceeds to effective charities, members maximize their giving impact and support organizations driving positive global change.

The Giving Pledge* (givingpledge.org)

A campaign encouraging wealthy individuals and families to commit more than half of their wealth to philanthropy, the Giving Pledge was created by Bill and Melinda Gates and Warren Buffett in 2010. It aims to shift social norms of philanthropy toward giving more, giving sooner, and giving smarter. Pledgers commit to donating the majority of their wealth to philanthropic causes either during their lifetime or in their will. The Giving Pledge is a moral commitment, not a legal contract, and doesn't involve pooling money or supporting specific causes.

*Note: The Giving Pledge is only open to those with a net worth exceeding $1 billion.

Network focused

Effective Altruism (effectivealtruism.org)

A philosophical and social movement that applies evidence and reason to determine the most effective ways to benefit others, the idea encourages individuals to consider all causes and actions, and to act in ways that bring about the greatest positive impact. Based on the simple but profound idea that we should do the most good possible with limited resources, the movement comprises a growing global community of people who care deeply about the world and strive to make it better through rigorous, scientific analyses of how to do the most good with their time and money.

P150 (p150.org)

A community built specifically for impact advisors that originally comprised the top 150 advisors, it has grown to include hundreds of members. The community features annual events, a highly active mailing list, and monthly meetups in key cities (London, New York, and San Francisco). Topics include deploying funding efficiently, utilizing different philanthropic vehicles, and sharing recommendations for specific projects.

Learning focused

AIM Grantmaking Program (aimgrantmaking.com)
The program for which this book was originally designed, AIM helps new and pivoting grantmakers achieve the highest impact possible. Multiple programs run each year with six to eight grantmakers who participate in a weekly book club culminating in a one-week, full-time, in-person training program. The program is free and aims to improve the philanthropic ecosystem as a whole. The graduate AIM community includes about 100 foundations and hosts events several times a year.

Forward Global (forward-global.org/en-uk)
A community of philanthropists, impact investors, and social entrepreneurs committed to advancing sustainable development and social impact globally, the network provides a way for members to connect. It offers a platform for sharing ideas and best practices, and collaborating on funding opportunities that support innovative solutions to global challenges like poverty, inequality, and climate change. Forward Global hosts regular events and workshops, focusing on identifying and supporting high-impact initiatives with the potential to drive systemic change.

Human/global health

Events focused

Skoll World Forum (skoll.org/skoll-world-forum)
This is an annual conference bringing together social entrepreneurs, innovators, investors, and thought leaders from around the world to share ideas, collaborate, and inspire action toward solving pressing global problems. Organized by the Skoll Foundation (founded by Jeff Skoll to support social entrepreneurs driving large-scale change), the forum offers a platform for attendees to connect, learn from experts, and explore new approaches to creating social impact. The forum also features the Skoll Awards for Social Entrepreneurship, which recognize outstanding social entrepreneurs.

OC Global (ocimpact.com/oc-global)
The international network of philanthropists, impact investors, and social entrepreneurs committed to promoting sustainable development and social impact

allows members to connect, share ideas, and collaborate on funding opportunities. OC Global hosts events and workshops to facilitate learning and focus on identifying and supporting innovative solutions to global challenges.

Giving focused

Global Health Funding Circle (globalhealthfunders.com)

A network of philanthropists, foundations, and impact investors committed to improving health outcomes in low- and middle-income countries, the circle is a way for members to connect and support organizations addressing global health challenges such as infectious diseases, maternal and child health, and healthcare access.

The Life You Can Save (thelifeyoucansave.org)

This nonprofit organization is committed to effective giving and reducing extreme poverty. Founded by philosopher Peter Singer, who argues that people in affluent countries have a moral obligation to donate to effective charities helping those in extreme poverty, the organization provides resources to help individuals make informed giving decisions. This includes recommending highly effective charities and a pledge program encouraging income percentage commitments. The organization also raises awareness about the impact of effective giving on reducing global poverty and suffering.

Network focused

Big Bang Philanthropy (bigbangphilanthropy.org)

This community of philanthropists supports high-risk, high-reward initiatives in the Global South with potential for transformative social impact. Founded by tech entrepreneurs and investors applying venture capital principles to philanthropy, members pool efforts to fund early-stage, innovative social impact projects that could scale and create systemic change.

Kokoro (kokorochange.com)

This global community of young philanthropists and changemakers is committed to creating a more just, sustainable, and compassionate world. The organization provides a platform for members to share ideas and resources, plus hosts events, workshops, and leadership development programs supporting members' personal and professional growth as changemakers.

Animals/environment

Events focused

Animal and Vegan Summit (avasummit.com)

An annual conference (with smaller, more frequent gatherings happening, too), the summit brings together activists, entrepreneurs, and thought leaders to promote animal rights, veganism, and plant-based living. It features keynote speeches, panel discussions, and workshops on topics including animal advocacy, plant-based nutrition, and the environmental impact of animal agriculture. The summit welcomes anyone interested in learning about animal rights and veganism, regardless of experience or involvement level.

The Conduit (theconduit.com)

This community of individuals and organizations committed to social change and sustainability serves as a hub for social impact, bringing together diverse change-makers such as entrepreneurs, investors, philanthropists, and activists. The Conduit maintains a physical coworking space in central London in the UK, hosting many philanthropic events, particularly environmentally focused ones.

Giving focused

Strategic Animal Funding Circle (animalfundingcircle.com)

This network of philanthropists and foundations is committed to promoting animal welfare and reducing animal suffering. It works to improve animals' lives in areas such as factory farming, animal testing, and wildlife conservation.

Resource Justice Network (resourcejustice.co.uk)

A community of organizations and individuals committed to promoting equitable access to natural resources and sustainable resource management that advocates for policies and practices promoting resource justice and sustainability.

Network focused

Senterra Funders (senterrafunders.org)

This is a network of philanthropists and foundations committed to reducing animal suffering and promoting a more humane and sustainable food system, bringing together members who work to improve farmed animals' lives through advocacy, research, and corporate engagement.

Environmental Funders Network (greenfunders.org)

A community of foundations and donors committed to advancing environmental sustainability and conservation, the network provides a platform for members to support organizations working to protect the environment and combat climate change. It also serves as a resource for environmental philanthropists, providing research, analysis, and thought leadership on emerging issues and trends in the field.

Other areas (e.g., social justice)

Events focused

Edge Funders Alliance (edgefunders.org)

This community of foundations and philanthropic organizations is committed to supporting systemic change and social justice movements, conducting research and advocacy to promote more equitable and sustainable funding practices in philanthropy.

Human Rights Funders Network (hrfn.org)

A global network of donors and grantmakers committed to advancing human rights through philanthropy, the network conducts research and advocacy to promote more effective and sustainable human rights funding practices.

Giving focused

Generation Pledge (generationpledge.org)

This is a community of young people who have pledged to give a portion of their income to effective charities throughout their lives. Members believe that by making a lifelong commitment to giving, they can create a significant positive impact and inspire others to do the same. Generation Pledge provides resources and support to help members make informed giving decisions and hosts events and workshops connecting members with each other and with experts in effective altruism and philanthropy.

Bolder Giving (boldergiving.org)

A nonprofit organization that inspires and supports people to give more, risk more, and inspire more, it provides resources, workshops, and support to help individuals and families unlock their full giving potential and maximize their philanthropic impact. Bolder Giving's mission is to create a community of givers committed to transforming the world through their generosity. There are no specific membership criteria; the organization works with individuals and families at all giving levels interested in deepening their philanthropy commitment.

Network focused

Resource Generation (resourcegeneration.org)

This is a nonprofit organization that organizes young people with wealth and class privilege to become transformative leaders working toward the equitable distribution of wealth, land, and power. The organization provides training, community organizing, and support to help members align their resources with their values and take action toward social justice. Membership is open to individuals aged 18-35 who self-identify as having wealth, class privilege, or access to intergenerational wealth.

Ariadne Network (ariadne-network.eu)

A European community of funders committed to supporting social change and human rights, the network provides a platform for members to share resources about efforts in Europe and beyond. Ariadne hosts regular events and workshops to facilitate peer learning and collaboration among members.

Building your community, in a nutshell

- A community is essential to both maintain and increase your long-term impact.

- You are likely already a member and connected to many others who could have more of an impact with your help. Keep in mind your highest impact might be from supporting others getting involved in grantmaking.

- There are tons of philanthropic communities focused on everything from events to specific-cause areas.

- The more impact-minded folks you connect with and spend time with, the better your grants will get.

Conclusion

Build your core well, and your impact can last a long time.

Building Brick by Brick

One way to think of building a foundation is to compare it to building a home. Some of us start from a blank canvas, open to creating anything, while others inherit structures that need significant renovations to make them fit their vision and values.

The first consideration when building a home is typically location, which affects its value and suitability. The equivalent for a foundation is picking your scope (geographic focus, cause area, and organization size). Just as a perfect house in a terrible location loses much of its value, some choices are still clearly suboptimal, like building beside a swamp or an airport (though scope is more subjective than many other aspects of grantmaking).

Remember the six grantmaking POWERS principles? They are much like the principles for building a home:

- **Price tag:** Knowing the cost and budget of the build
- **Options:** Considering different designs and materials
- **Who**: Determining who to contract to build the house
- **Evaluate:** Comparing the plans to other houses you've admired
- **Reduce:** Minimizing your time on unimportant details (otherwise, even a simple renovation becomes a full-time job)
- **Substance:** Building a home that will stand the test of time

And even with an ideal house in a beautiful location, the neighbors make a huge difference, as a community can make a place feel like a refuge or a constant struggle. These core principles apply whether you're building a tiny cabin or a mansion, just as they apply to foundations of any size or focus.

You want to connect with others already in the same neighborhood (related grantmaking communities) while also inviting those you already know into your home (leveraging your network). Both approaches build truly meaningful connections.

And much like building a home, creating a foundation takes work, but it is uniquely satisfying when you see the results of hundreds of thoughtful decisions.

We all want impact that lasts, regardless of whether we're a spend-down foundation or one planned to exist in perpetuity. Like houses, foundations need tune-ups and repairs, but if you get the core right, your long-term work becomes much easier. Great homes and foundations can both set trends and, when well-positioned, become powerful sources of community and purpose.

Two Model Architects: Field-Leading Foundations

1) Coefficient Giving: the grand design

Coefficient Giving[25] (previously known as Open Philanthropy) stands out as one of the most impressive grantmakers in the field. Backed by dozens of full-time staff members and years of operation, it brings an exceptional level of rigor to its work. It can dive deeper than many other foundations and, importantly, shares its findings and grants transparently with other grantmakers.

How does this philanthropic powerhouse measure up on our framework?

Scope: Coefficient Giving has selected clear focus areas where it's often a major player, frequently contributing at least 10% of its chosen spaces' total funding. It lists these areas publicly, making it easy for potential grantees to determine if they fit. Within narrower areas (like factory farming), it doesn't restrict itself by geography or organization size, while in broader areas (like global health), it often narrows to specific countries and implementation partners.

Grantmaking POWERS:

- **Price tag**: Coefficient Giving consistently requests cost-effectiveness data, and for larger grants, even builds internal models to evaluate this crucial information.

- **Options**: While not publicly disclosed, its published data suggests it funds only the top 10-20% of opportunities considered.

- **Who**: Given its substantial annual giving (hundreds of millions), it's built extensive in-house capacity with a dedicated team of experts.

- **Evaluate**: It maintains clear internal benchmarks, often directly comparing potential grants against successful past investments.

- **Reduce**: Despite its large grants, it typically respects NGOs' time, aligning with the guideline of about an hour or less per $50K granted.

- **Substance**: Its due diligence focuses on substantive, analytical, and quantifiable questions. While it considers leadership and risk profiles, its primary concern is expected cost-effectiveness and overall impact.

I'd give it a 5.5/6 on our POWERS checklist!

Community: Coefficient Giving participates in numerous philanthropic communities, from small groups in which it's the largest funder to larger networks where it's one member among many. It belongs to many of the communities mentioned throughout this book and even helped establish several of them. It leverages its position effectively, recently leading a $100-million co-funding initiative for lead elimination, contributing the first 20% alone while bringing in network partners for the remaining 80%.

Overall: Coefficient Giving demonstrates how these principles operate successfully at a large scale.

2) The Global Focus Foundation: the boutique builder

The Global Focus Foundation (a pseudonym) represents the other end of the spectrum, with just one staff member. This foundation exemplifies thoughtful, modest grantmaking. One advantage of its small size is agility. I've seen it fund promising opportunities that others later recognized as brilliant, but couldn't move quickly enough to support.

Scope: True to its name, this funder maintains intense focus. While its cause areas have evolved over time, it becomes fully immersed once a direction is chosen, attending conferences, consulting experts, and funding multiple organizations in related areas. Some charities even seek the advice of Global Focus on matters outside their funding scope.

Grantmaking POWERS:

- **Price tag**: Extremely price-sensitive, it benchmarks costs against others in the space and directly communicates to charities when proposals seem particularly good or poor value.

- **Options**: As part of a funding circle (that I also belong to), it reviews hundreds of applications and receives direct referrals from peer funders.

- **Who**: It develops deep expertise alone but also engages philanthropic advisors when entering new areas or focusing on specialized sub-sectors.

- **Evaluate:** It has a concrete benchmark for each of the cause areas focused on.

- **Reduce**: Making grants in the $30,000–$300,000 range, it respects NGOs' time, typically requiring just one brief application and one call while conducting deeper research independently.

- **Substance**: Its rapid response sometimes means using style as a proxy, as deep substantive evaluation takes time, which is not always available.

I give it a 5/6 on our checklist!

Community: This grantmaker actively participates in several funding circles and larger movements. They generously share what they know while remaining transparent about knowledge gaps. It often elevates the groups it joins, improving outcomes for everyone involved. With the unique advantage of being a relatively seasoned grantmaker who still embraces modern evidence and philanthropic trends, it's become an invaluable contact for newer donors in their demographic.

Overall: The Global Focus Foundation demonstrates that even small foundations can create an outsized impact through nimble grantmaking and community influence.

Building your legacy

Neither grantmaker is perfect. Both have funded initiatives that they later regretted. Coefficient Giving has acknowledged moving too slowly in certain areas (a common challenge for large funders), while the Global Focus Foundation has occasionally backed ineffective grantees. Both of these grantmakers genuinely strive to maximize good with their available resources and have achieved remarkable results. Together, funders like these create an ecosystem worth more than the sum of its parts.

Your foundation can likewise apply these tools in unique ways that help you become a successful member of the broader philanthropic community. Your mission is to create a massive impact you can look back on with pride.

Think about the most successful grantmakers we've met throughout this book. They weren't necessarily the wealthiest or the most experienced. Rather, they were the ones who approached their philanthropy with both heart and head: compassion paired with rigor, enthusiasm matched with evidence, and personal values aligned with strategic thinking.

Remember Lake and Ryan from our opening story? The ideal grantmaker combines Lake's genuine compassion with Ryan's analytical mind. Similarly, think about the contrast between John and Sarah; one consumed grantees' time with endless demands, while the other respected their partners' resources and focused her own effort on due diligence. These weren't just illustrative anecdotes; they represent real differences of approach to grantmaking and the real choices you'll face in your giving journey.

Your Next Steps

This is just the beginning. Here's how to move forward with confidence:

- **Define your scope**: Choose a focus area where your funding could reasonably represent 2–20% of the field (e.g., cause area, organization size, geography). *Example: "I will focus on global health organizations with sub-$1M budgets working in Sub-Saharan Africa."*

- **Apply the POWERS principles**: Start with just one or two that resonate most strongly with you, then gradually incorporate the others.

- **Pick your community**: Join a funding circle aligned with your cause area. Make a public commitment like the Founders' Pledge. Choose one conference this year where you'll meet peers and learn more.

- **Learn more**: Explore our appendices for deeper dives into specific topics, or consider the AIM Grantmaking Course for additional guidance. (impactfulgrantmaking.com) [26]

Most importantly, begin. The journey to more effective giving starts with a single thoughtful grant. By combining compassion with rigor, you can create an impact that transforms not just the lives of those you help but your own experience as a philanthropist.

Finally, remember that we started this journey because great philanthropy saves lives, sometimes hundreds or thousands of them. With the principles and communities we've explored together, you're now equipped to create that impact yourself.

Your giving can do twice as much good! So go ahead. The world is waiting.

Appendix: Guide

Our appendix offers deeper, more academic treatments of topics covered in the main book. If you want to explore a chapter further or need additional clarity, the related appendix is often the best place to start.

Appendix A: Recommended Resources

Some of the most important resources are the communities that we recommended checking out earlier in the chapter *Connect*. The following list is primarily focused on enhancing your information or knowledge base.

Recommended books	Why we recommend it
Enlightenment Now, by Steven Pinker	A hugely influential and surprising book that argues the case that the world is getting better. Highly relevant for all grantmakers and foundations to know the trend of how the world is progressing.
How to Measure Anything, by Douglas Hubbard	Though fairly technical, this is one of the best books about how to measure things that are typically difficult to quantify. Particularly a good fit for grantmakers in hard-to-evaluate areas.
Crucial Conversations, by Kerry Patterson et al.	This is the best book about how to communicate better in key conversations, particularly philanthropic ones with family members. Most useful for grantmakers who have the ability to leverage more impact.

The Life You Can Save, by Peter Singer	Great introduction to ethics; compellingly lays out the case for why and how we can take action to provide immense benefit to others, at minimal cost to ourselves.
Animal Liberation, by Peter Singer	This book was significant to the founding growth of animal welfare as a philanthropic area and describes why animals are worthy of moral consideration. It has inspired a worldwide movement to eliminate factory farms.
Talent, by Tyler Cowen	Great introduction to early-stage hiring and how to find great talent at the start of an organization's life cycle.

Recommended articles & videos	Why we recommend it
"GiveWell as moneyball"[27]	This 2024 article, published on the GiveWell nonprofit's blog, explains how quantitative methods can be used to find undervalued charities in a similar way to sports teams using advanced analytics.
"Reasoning Transparency"[28]	Published on the Open Philanthropy website in 2017, this article clearly describes the benefits of transparent reasoning, particularly for grantmakers and charity reviewers.
"Principles for Success"[29]	This 30-minute video from the YouTube channel of economist Ray Dalio summarizes his *New York Times* best-seller, *Principles,* about how to use feedback and succeed at your goals.
"Drive: The truth about what motivates us"[30]	A TED Talk by Dan Pink summarizes research about how important it is to have a purpose and what really motivates people to work efficiently.
"Why farmed animals?"[31]	A video/article from Animal Charity Evaluators about why farmed animals are worth considering instead of companion animals.

Appendix B: Theory of Change for Foundations

A Theory of Change is the nonprofit world's equivalent of a business model. It explains how an organization or project plans to create impact and why that approach is expected to work. Just as investors usually require a business plan before providing capital, foundations may only consider projects that can show a clear and convincing Theory of Change.

For a foundation, the Theory of Change serves as both a roadmap and a test of logic. It traces the steps between a grantee's actions and the long-term results they hope to achieve. A good Theory of Change begins with **inputs** and **activities**, the specific actions that aim to create change, such as distributing bed nets. These actions lead to **outputs**, the direct and measurable results, such as people gaining access to nets. Next come the intermediate **outcomes**, the short- and medium-term effects that connect outputs to the final goal, such as regular use of nets and lower malaria rates. The final stage is the **impact**, the lasting change in people's lives or in society, such as improved health or lives saved.

When reviewing proposals, foundations should look for Theories of Change that show clear reasoning and a strong understanding of the problem. A thoughtful plan reflects knowledge of the people affected, the systems they live in, and the barriers that stand in the way of progress. It also shows that the organization has reasoned backward from its desired impact to the specific steps needed to reach it, with each step supported by logic or evidence.

The strongest Theories of Change share several traits. They focus on a coherent set of activities instead of a scattered mix of programs. They identify the evidence or assumptions behind each link in the chain. They show how confident the organization is in each step. They also make it clear who is responsible for taking action at every stage.

Foundations should also recognize the warning signs of a weak Theory of Change. These include stopping short of the ultimate goal, skipping over key steps, grouping several outcomes into one vague statement, treating the plan as a one-time exercise, or failing to connect it to monitoring and learning.

When foundations encourage grantees to build and update strong Theories of Change, they help those organizations clarify their strategies and measure their results. In turn, the foundation itself gains better insight into what works and how its funding contributes to real, lasting change.

There are two ways in which theories of change play a significant role in grantmaking foundations' decision-making:

1. Assessing grantees

2. Defining a theory of change for the foundation itself

Assessing grantees

Grantmakers should expect every potential grantee to have a theory of change for their organization or project, or be able to produce one when asked. Funders need to hold the organizations they fund, meaning the people doing the work, accountable for using a clear, realistic, evidence-based plan to turn dollars into impact.

Better yet, grantmakers should expect that recipient organizations use their theory of change to identify priorities for their monitoring and evaluation (M&E) plan, and that they build a cost-effectiveness analysis based on the theory of change's structure: quantifying the costs of their inputs, as well as the size and probability of the desired outputs, outcomes, and impact.

Theory of change for the foundation

It may be a little less intuitive, but a second way that theories of change come into play is in a foundation's decision-making, articulating the strategy for how the foundation itself will have impact.

Direct impact of grantmaking

At first thought, it might seem that there would be one theory of change for how all foundations have impact: "We fund impactful activities." In this sense, a foundation's theory of change is the sum of each of its grantees, with an additional input at the beginning:

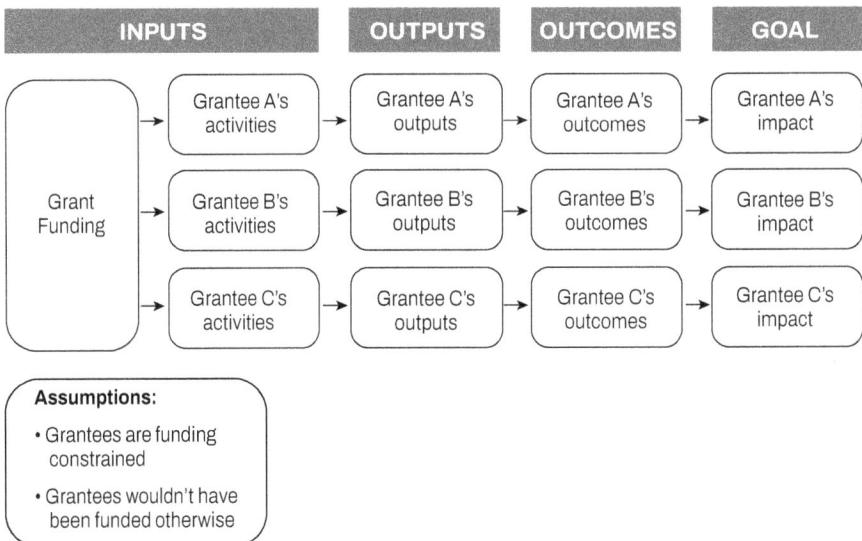

INPUTS	OUTPUTS	OUTCOMES	GOAL
	Grantee A's activities	Grantee A's outputs	Grantee A's outcomes	Grantee A's impact
Grant Funding	Grantee B's activities	Grantee B's outputs	Grantee B's outcomes	Grantee B's impact
	Grantee C's activities	Grantee C's outputs	Grantee C's outcomes	Grantee C's impact

Assumptions:
- Grantees are funding constrained
- Grantees wouldn't have been funded otherwise

In some cases, foundations can define their theory of change in terms of a specific problem (e.g., inhumane chicken farming) or a specific type of solution (e.g., plant-based alternatives) that they have decided to focus on, where the theory of change reflects their view of the best strategy for how to improve the world within this focus area:

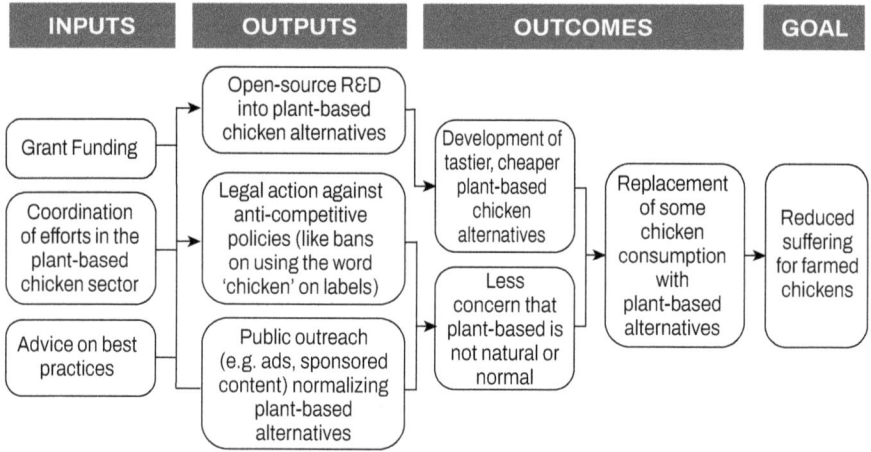

INPUTS	OUTPUTS	OUTCOMES	GOAL

Grant Funding → Open-source R&D into plant-based chicken alternatives

Coordination of efforts in the plant-based chicken sector → Legal action against anti-competitive policies (like bans on using the word 'chicken' on labels)

Advice on best practices → Public outreach (e.g. ads, sponsored content) normalizing plant-based alternatives

→ Development of tastier, cheaper plant-based chicken alternatives

Less concern that plant-based is not natural or normal

→ Replacement of some chicken consumption with plant-based alternatives

→ Reduced suffering for farmed chickens

Armed with this kind of strategically framed theory of change, foundations can seek grantees who can make a contribution and publicly communicate how other organizations can play a role in realizing their vision. The downside of this type of theory of change for a foundation is that it forces you to have a clear and narrow view of the problem you will focus on and how it can best be solved. As a result, this approach isn't suitable for all foundations, and when foundations do take this approach, they should be mindful not to become anchored to one narrow view of how to improve the world.

Indirect foundation impact

In addition to the direct impact of providing funding, a foundation can also have a broader impact through **thought leadership**. For example, you might publish research (like Coefficient Giving's reports on different cause areas), write blog posts (like the Mulago Foundation), develop impact metrics (like Charity Entrepreneurship's Welfare Points), or create public cost-effectiveness analyses of charities and interventions (like GiveWell).

Foundations can also have an impact by influencing their network (which may include other high-net-worth individuals, or even other foundations) to give more, or give more effectively. Foundations can create leverage in several ways, effectively multiplying their spending, including by accessing government funding. Strategies for creating leverage are discussed earlier in the book.

Another way to have an impact is by setting good norms in the nonprofit sector, making it a public policy only to fund organizations that follow certain best practices (like, for example, pre-committing to shut down if the M&E doesn't show a predetermined threshold of cost-effectiveness).

Meanwhile, it is overly narrow to only consider the impact of grant dollars in terms of the inputs they fund. For example, sometimes when a foundation gives a grant to an early-stage organization, that makes the difference between it going insolvent and surviving long enough to scale into a massively impactful charity (like the Against Malaria Foundation). By ensuring the longevity of a highly impactful charity, the grant's impact extends beyond the immediate activities it covers, contributing to a significant percentage of the organization's long-term good work. Similarly, foundations can be active in their grantmaking, influencing how many and what type of projects come into existence. They are then partially responsible for the lifetime impact of those projects, beyond the activities they fund directly.

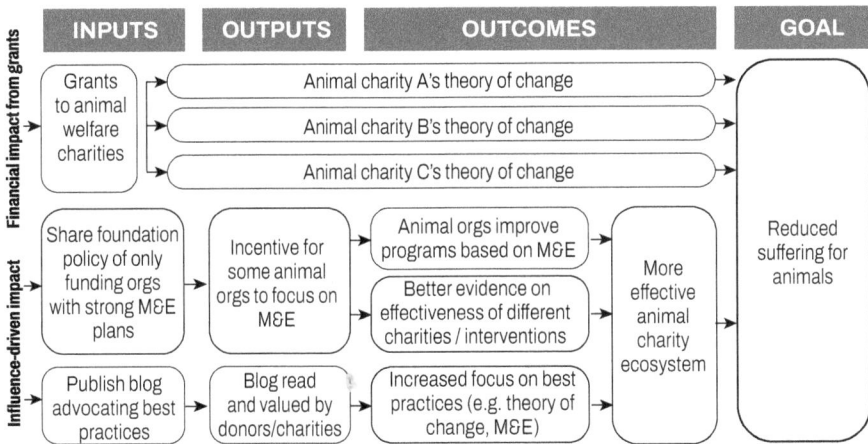

In some cases, the indirect impact of these grants can be significantly larger than their direct impact! But the chances of this being the case accidentally are low and it takes thought and effort. For this reason, we encourage foundations to define their own theory of change, so that they make a conscious decision about which of these other forms of impact they will work to cultivate.

Appendix C: Cost-Effectiveness Analysis

Role in your toolkit

When we need to produce a single numerical output from the information we have, we typically reach for a calculator. Cost-effectiveness analyses (CEAs) are the grantmaker's calculator. Commonly used in economics, health policymaking, and charity evaluation, CEAs calculate the ratio of the cost of a given action or intervention relative to its modeled impact. Cost is usually measured in dollars, with impact measured in concrete terms (e.g., lives saved) or more abstract ones (like Disability-Adjusted Life Years).

Imagine two charities that have been modeled with a CEA. One can train a guide dog to assist one blind person for each additional $1,000 donated. The other can perform one vision-restoring cataract surgery for each additional $35 donated. While these are two very different interventions, because they are both fundamentally aimed at alleviating blindness, we can use cost-effectiveness analyses to decide that funding cataract surgeries is a far more efficient way to achieve that goal.[32]

CEAs are a particularly useful item in a grantmaker's toolkit because they can aggregate all of the information about an intervention, such as the results of scientific studies, probabilities, and scenarios from experts, and heuristics like replaceability, into a single number. This allows you to easily compare interventions with each other. But, like a calculator, the CEA's single numerical output tends to inspire a greater sense of trust than can be justified. After all, a calculator's outputs are only as good as the quality of its inputs, and its calculations are very sensitive to user error. Therefore, you should check your own and others' calculations twice, and sense-check the results against trusted data points.

Cost-effectiveness estimates should play an important but limited role in grantmaking decisions. It is important to distinguish between the true cost-effectiveness of an action and the modeled cost-effectiveness. The true cost-effectiveness of an action, if known, could be weighted very heavily when making a decision. However, we generally lack important data about the world and have various uncertainties. The closest we can usually get to the true cost-effectiveness of an intervention is through constructing a model, which is an imperfect estimate. That's why it's important to remember the saying, "all models are wrong, but some are useful."

Sadly, low-evidence CEAs are almost always overly optimistic and regress to the mean when further depth is put into them. This is part of why both GiveWell and CE are far less excited about a highly speculative CEA that looks promising than one that has been conducted more thoroughly. Given their limitations, it is important to only use CEAs in conjunction with other methodologies, looking for options that appear strong from multiple perspectives. We expect CEAs to be particularly useful in areas with large quantitative differences, where our other evaluative criteria are less reliable, and where objective data and strong evidence are available.

Strengths and weaknesses

Strengths

Enables comparison of options in terms of impact, our fundamental goal: Ultimately, the question ambitious foundations need to answer is how to have the most impact possible with finite financial resources. A CEA may be an imperfect model, but it speaks directly to our key question by quantifying the impact-per-dollar of each option so that we can choose the best one. Out of all of our decision-making tools, it has the clearest theoretical correlation with having done well, even if model errors weaken it in practice.

Enables formal sensitivity analysis: A sensitivity analysis can locate the most important assumptions, variables, and considerations affecting the endline conclusion: the factors that could most radically change the amount of good achieved. Formal sensitivity analysis can be done quickly and easily on a CEA, showing the key parameters that are the most important to get right.[33]

Transparency: With all the variables and formulae on display, an outsider can tell what factors are reflected in the output, and how. Meanwhile, with each variable clearly quantified and sources attributed, an outsider can understand what evidence the decision is based on and where assumptions are being made. This makes it easier for them to sense-check the decision and to understand why it might deviate from their own.

Scope sensitive: Humans are notoriously bad at properly understanding scope,[34] so it's a major concern that many non-CEA models don't explicitly reflect it. An expert may tell us that one intervention is "far, far better" in one dimension than another intervention, but unless we explicitly quantify that in a model, we're unlikely to capture the very significant difference between being 100x better or 1,000x better in that dimension.

Weaknesses

Individual CEAs are vulnerable to errors: Most CEAs are structured as linear calculations, such that a single error can massively distort the outcome. For example, GiveWell once found five separate errors in a Disease Control Priorities DALY figure for deworming that contributed to an overestimation of the intervention's cost-effectiveness by 100 times.[35]

Individual CEAs are error-prone: Single errors are common, even among the most rigorous modelers (see the example above). In fact, because rigorous modelers tend to produce more thorough and complex models, their models have a greater number of variables and formulae in which to make errors, and it is more difficult to find these errors.

Aggregating CEAs is particularly vulnerable to errors: Perhaps even more concerning than the risk that individual CEAs contain errors is the risk that those CEAs end up guiding decisions. When decision-makers who are optimizing for cost-effectiveness review the outcomes of many CEAs, they select outliers from the option set. But outliers can be caused by both outlier cost-effectiveness and modeling errors. Depending on the underlying distributions, this can result in optimizers systematically selecting for results with errors (a formally proven phenomenon called the "optimizer's curse"). Overweighting CEAs in our decision-making could lead us to neglect good opportunities that have fewer favorable errors.

Slow: Properly creating or reviewing a CEA is very time-consuming, especially compared with weighted-factor models (another method for aggregating evidence discussed in this section).

It can depend heavily on subjective value judgments: It is surprising how much value judgments can differ. For example, GiveWell assumes that the "value of averting the death of an individual under 5 [years of age]" is 50 times larger than the value of "doubling consumption for one person for one year."[36] Reasonable estimates could vary by a factor of 10 in both directions. The best CEAs make these value judgements explicit and allow users to edit them to match their own values. Nonetheless, it means that the results of many CEAs can't be generalized; they need to be understood with reference to the underlying values of the modeler. This makes comparisons between the results of CEAs from different organizations particularly fraught.

Inefficient at capturing multiple effects, so often neglect indirect effects: CEAs work well when the majority of an intervention's costs and benefits come from a single direct effect. Unfortunately, effort scales roughly linearly with the number of additional effects we model. Meanwhile, indirect effects are often more complicated to model and numerous than direct ones. As a result, CEAs are less efficient at modeling interventions that are effective via a number of effects (like family planning, which likely influences maternal health, children's health, family economic outcomes, animal welfare, and environmental outcomes). In the end, these more complicated interventions end up having a smaller percentage of their cost and benefit included in the model, leading to unfair comparisons with interventions that have simpler effects.

Concerns with reliance on CEAs in charity evaluation have been discussed in depth elsewhere. For further reading, we recommend GiveWell's discussion of the theoretical concerns[37] and Saulius Šimčikas's exposition of practical concerns.[38]

Creating CEAs vs. reviewing others' CEAs

It's best practice for most foundations to incorporate formal cost-effectiveness analysis into grantmaking decisions, especially those involving large amounts of funding. But should you do the cost-effectiveness analysis yourself, or review the work of others? There are significant trade-offs involved in this decision.

Costs of self-creating CEAs

Slower speed: While reviewing a CEA properly is time-consuming in its own right, creating one from scratch is generally far slower. This can be a problem when you have a time-sensitive funding decision to make.

Higher cost: The labor-intensive process of creating a CEA results in high costs. Even if your organization is willing to devote the capacity to creating a CEA, you may not actually have the capability in-house, in which case you'll need to develop it, hire it, or pay an independent third party to create it on your behalf. This last option entails many of the costs associated with reviewing the existing CEAs of others.

Less access to information (sometimes): As an outsider, you'll typically have poorer access to primary data on an intervention than those conducting the intervention themselves. To the extent that you are reliant on others to provide you with that data, you are exposed to the risk that they cherry-pick data that will lead you to judge them favorably. Of course, this only applies to interventions that are already being implemented; if it's a new idea, you may be in just as good a position as the implementing organization.

Benefits of self-creating

Better incentives: Organizations seeking funding have an incentive to arrive at positive conclusions when analyzing their own cost-effectiveness. Even well-meaning organizations that seem to have impact as their primary goal are susceptible to bias. This applies less when using the CEA of an independent organization like GiveWell or an academic, but you should still be mindful of their incentives.

Avoids adopting others' implicit assumptions: High-quality CEAs will make their assumptions as explicit as possible, but no CEA is perfect. As a result, using the CEAs of others often means adopting their implicit assumptions, unless you're able to catch them during the review process. These assumptions can be about the facts; for example, an independent reviewer of GiveWell's CEA of unconditional cash transfers found that they were implicitly assuming that the portion of cash transfers that isn't invested is consumed in one year.[39] These assumptions can also be moral ones, like assigning no value to changes in the number of people who will be born, or epistemological ones, like how to account for uncertainty about future outcomes. When creating the CEA yourself, you may still forget to make all of your assumptions explicit, but at least the result will reflect your own assumptions, and not those of another organization. It is also important to remember that everyone in your own organization will have different implicit assumptions, and even if you hire people with similar beliefs to your own, there will be differences you need to be aware of.

Contributes to greater diversity of perspectives: Cost-effectiveness analysis is challenging, resulting in relatively few analyses of any given intervention, and even fewer high-quality analyses. This makes the philanthropic sector more vulnerable to poor resource-allocation decisions caused by a single error in one influential CEA. Creating new CEAs not only increases the likelihood of identifying errors in existing CEAs but also enhances the philanthropic sector's resilience against individual errors.

So, should you create or review? As with most things, no one answer makes sense for everyone. However, one piece of universal guidance we can give is: do not prematurely rule out creating your own. We have observed that people tend to underestimate how much work is involved in properly reviewing others' CEAs, leading them to choose this option more often than they should. In reality, properly reviewing others' CEAs isn't that much less costly than creating a CEA yourself, so you should consider this as a real option. You can also use others' CEAs as a way to save time coming up with potential structures and data sources.

Best practices for creating CEAs

When creating a CEA, the key is to start really simple, with a small number of very well-cited variables. Factors like the cost of an organization and the number of beneficiaries helped are often easy numbers to find good evidence on. The size of the benefit per beneficiary (e.g., how much using a bed net helps people) will be much harder, but can be drawn from academic literature. Creating a good CEA is beyond the scope of this book, but we have some detailed resources on it at: **www.charityentrepreneurship.com/foundation-program-handbook**

Best practices for reviewing CEAs

One way to review third-party CEAs is to vet them for accuracy and then use their results as they are, without significantly building upon the CEA yourself. Some best practices for how to do this, which you can do to varying degrees of rigor, include:

Check whether you agree with the assumptions: You may need to adjust them to reflect your organization's views. Ensure that when you're comparing the results of two different CEAs, they're using compatible assumptions.

Conduct an evidence audit: Look at the references for each value in the analysis. Do the values in the model actually match the underlying literature? There may have been a mistake in interpretation or even in transcribing the values. Is the literature generalizable to the context that the CEA is for, or are there relevant differences between the populations, geographies, or interventions? When conducting this evidence audit, you should prioritize the variables to which the model's results are most sensitive.

Conduct a formula audit: Simple formula errors are common, even among the best CEAs,[40] and are a greater risk the more complicated the model is. A quick way to do an audit is to change a variable and see if the model moves in the direction it should (e.g., if you raise the cost, does the cost-effectiveness, in fact, go down?). You would be shocked at how often this turns up an error.

Question whether the results hold up at scale: Instead of taking it as a given that the cost-effectiveness would remain constant if the intervention was conducted at a larger or smaller scale, consider this first: Should you expect diminishing returns? Should you expect economies of scale? Are there limiting factors that would constrain the scale at which this cost-effectiveness applies, e.g., due to limited talent who can do the job?

Make sure you know what is and isn't included: Almost no CEA will be fully exhaustive in terms of the costs and benefits included. This is fine, so long as you're aware of what is and isn't included, so that you can make fair comparisons of different interventions. In general, the more rigorous a CEA is, the less cost-effective it will find the intervention to be, as additional factors tend to mean more costs or discounted benefits. Inclusions/exclusions to look for:[41]

MISSING COSTS:

- Does the analysis include the cost of fundraising? There can be vast differences in how much time and money different cause areas/interventions need to invest in fundraising. Some spend a huge amount of time applying for small grants, while others only solicit one big grant, for instance.

- Does the analysis include the cost of evaluation? Funders for different cause areas hold charities to very different M&E standards. The actual cost of conducting M&E varies dramatically for different interventions.

- Does the analysis include past and future costs? A homeless charity may have already spent huge amounts on housing, but is only counting its future costs in its cost-effectiveness analysis. Its cost-effectiveness would therefore be greatly exaggerated. Similarly, a charity that conducts corporate cage-free egg campaigns may only count the cost of achieving the cage-free commitments and fail to mention the future cost of enforcing those commitments. This would also greatly influence how cost-effective their intervention appears.

MISSING INDIRECT EFFECTS:

- What indirect benefits are included? If you compare malaria bed net distribution to a family-planning intervention, the former looks better when considering impact on human health alone. But if you also consider the impact on animal welfare and the climate, family planning may come out on top.

- Are there indirect costs that aren't being included? If you distribute a certain product or offer a service, what does that do to local markets? What do cash transfers do to local inflation?

MISSING COUNTERFACTUALS:

- Most CEAs fail to consider the counterfactual cost of inputs. For example, if those involved in the intervention would have been doing something else that's impactful if the intervention didn't exist, then the opportunity cost should be included for maximum accuracy. If the intervention's likely funders would otherwise be funding something else impactful, then that lost impact is an additional cost. If other actors bear some costs for the intervention (e.g., if the government has to spend money enforcing a policy), then you need to include what those resources would have otherwise been used for.

- You also need to consider counterfactuals on the benefits side: If a charity hadn't done the intervention, would things have eventually improved anyway, or would nothing have changed? For example, if LEEP hadn't convinced the government of Malawi to pass and enforce regulations against leaded paint, the government probably would have done so of its own accord eventually; the benefit only comes from speeding it up.

Best practices for improving CEAs

Do your own thinking before looking at the model: Consider how your model ought to be structured, what variables are likely to be important, and what kind of assumptions and outcomes might be reasonable *before* you look at the model. That way, you avoid the risk of being drawn in by the other model's juicy results and influenced by its key features. By thinking through structure, variables, and outcomes before you even open the model, you can dig deeper to understand whose approach is better if it winds up looking very different from what you had imagined.

Recreate the model in a new document: It's easy to fail to spot errors in a model when you are just building on it. We recommend recreating it in a new document so that you're less likely to reproduce the original author's errors. You may make errors of your own, but if you do, your results will deviate from the original (unless you make the exact same mistakes), which will prompt you to check your work to understand why. Recreating the model in a new document will also allow you to use a structure that is consistent with models you have for other interventions or organizations, allowing for easier cross-comparison.

Focus on the most sensitive, least evidenced variables: Prioritize efforts where they are likely to make the biggest adjustments to the model's output: on the variables that have the poorest evidence base and which the result is most sensitive to.

Add any missing factors that may change the outcome: If any of the factors listed on the previous pages are missing from the model, but seem likely to significantly impact the outcome, consider adding them.

Consider removing extraneous factors: All else equal, simple models are better. They're more readable and have fewer points of failure. If a model includes factors that significantly complicate it but make a negligible difference to the outcome (e.g., if a CEA for mosquito nets included the effect of solar eclipses on mosquito reproductive patterns), consider removing them. You could summarize their negligible impact somewhere, in case the question arises of why those factors weren't included, or you could save a version of the model that still includes those factors.

Choosing your output metrics

Use two types of output metrics

Straddling the border between a question about tools and a question about ethics is the question of what output metric to build our CEA around. CEAs should have two types of output metrics that serve two different purposes: concrete impact and abstract (i.e., general) impact.

Concrete impact metrics are things like "cost to prevent a case of malaria," "cost to save the life of a child under the age of 5," or "cost to avert a year of hen confinement in cages." These are comprehensible and intuitive, which makes them more useful for communicating to a broad audience, more motivating for those working on the intervention, and easier to sense-check (e.g., anyone can tell that if the CEA says it costs two cents to save a life, that's probably incorrect).

Abstract impact metrics are things like "cost per QALY (quality-adjusted life-year)" and "cost per DALY (disability-adjusted life-year)," which attempt to convert all sorts of different impacts into a common metric for the purposes of making comparisons between different interventions. These metrics are unintuitive, harder to sense-check (is saving a DALY for $20 plausible?), and fraught with weaknesses (see below). However, because they enable comparisons between interventions, they are an important part of a CEA.

Expressing cost-effectiveness with both types of metrics is a great way to avoid alienating anyone who disagrees with your way of distilling impact into an abstract metric. Some people might take issue with DALYs, but agree that curing a person of blindness is a meaningful measurement, for example. By using both concrete and abstract metrics, we reap the benefits of both while ensuring common ground on how to measure impact. This way, the most important conversations don't get cut short by distracting disagreements. Meanwhile, third parties have the option of converting the concrete metric to their abstract metric of choice.

Choosing your abstract metric

Which abstract impact metric should we use when making comparisons? Different fields and cause areas tend to use different metrics, which have their own unique strengths and weaknesses. First, let's go over the meaning of each.

Disability-adjusted life years (DALYs) represent the loss of the equivalent of one year of human life at full health. The metric captures both the potential years of life lost (YLL) due to premature death, and the equivalent years of healthy life lost due to living with a disability or illness (YLD).

- **Disability weights:** YLD is calculated by multiplying the length of time one experiences the disability or illness by a "disability weight," which attempts to capture how much the disability or illness affects the person. Disability weights are typically calculated using a method known as pairwise comparisons, where members of the public are given descriptions of two people's health states and asked who is healthier. Despite relying on subjective judgements, these judgements are quite convergent ($r \geq 0.9$ in all countries tested except one), even across countries in different continents and with vastly different income levels.[42] However, even if people's judgements are consistent, they risk being consistently mistaken, because they are based on what people imagine certain ailments to be like, and fail to consider that people seem to adapt psychologically to some conditions (e.g., blindness) far more than others (e.g., depression).[43]

- **Age weighting:** Once standard practice, it is now an optional extra step to assign different weights to DALYs lost at different ages. This step aims to capture the intuition that we value years lived as a young adult more than years lived as a newborn or elderly person. GiveWell uses an age weighting curve generated by taking a weighted average of the results from a survey of donors (60% weight), a survey of low-income people in Ghana and Kenya (30% weight), and the views of GiveWell staff (10% weight).[44] A challenge with using DALYs is that there is no way of comparing results calculated using age-weights to those calculated without or with different weights.

- **Time discounting**: Another optional feature of DALYs is to discount future benefits using a discount rate (e.g., 3%). Justifications for whether to use a discount rate and what value to choose are inconsistent.

Quality-adjusted life years (QALYs) represent the gain of the equivalent of one year of human life at full health. They are the predecessor of DALYs, and are often used interchangeably, despite having relevant differences:[45]

- **Opposite direction:** A positive number of QALYs represents health-years gained, while a positive number of DALYs represents health-years lost.

- **Allow for negative states:** QALYs allow for states worse than death (e.g., extreme pain); however, this capability isn't commonly or consistently used.

- **Range of disability weight methodologies:** Unlike DALYs, which have converged on pairwise comparisons as the primary method for generating disability weights, QALYs use a range of methods, including the time tradeoff, standard gamble, discrete choice experiments, visual analog scale, and person tradeoff methods.

- **Lack of central authority:** The Institute for Health Metrics and Evaluation (IHME) has applied DALYs to a wide range of scenarios in a sane and consistent way, which serves as a common source to inform different practitioners' analyses. Unfortunately, there is no real equivalent for QALYs.

Well-being-adjusted life years (WELLBYs) represent increasing the life satisfaction of one person by one point on a 10-point scale for one year.[46] They are a far newer and less widespread measure than QALYs or DALYs, which came into existence to address the complaints that existing metrics (a) focus only on health, which isn't all that matters to our welfare, (b) rely on the naive assessments of people who mostly haven't experienced the illnesses, and (c) generally don't account for the fact that certain outcomes can be worse than death.[47]

Welfare points, an invention of Charity Entrepreneurship, compare the well-being of different animals in a common unit.[48] This enables a comparison of different animal interventions and, theoretically, a comparison of interventions that benefit humans vs. animals. We say "theoretically" because Charity Entrepreneurship has not used welfare points this way; we conduct our research rounds by cause area, such that we don't need to compare interventions that benefit animals and humans.

However, welfare points could be used to make such comparisons and could even be converted into DALYs. Each welfare point represents a difference of 1 on a scale from +100 (an ideal life) to -100 (a completely unpleasant life), with 0 representing uncertainty about the life being net positive or negative. A human or animal life is assigned a welfare score[49] through a weighted average of eight criteria:

- Death rate/reason (20% weight)

- Human preference from behind the veil of ignorance (20% weight)

- Disease/injury/functional impairment (17% weight)

- Thirst/hunger/malnutrition (15% weight)

- Anxiety/fear/pain/distress (15% weight)

- Environmental challenge (5% weight)

- Index of biological markers, like cortisol and dopamine (4% weight)

- Behavioral/interactive restriction (4% weight)

We haven't yet published resources to enable other organizations to use our welfare point system for decision-making in a way that would be consistent with how we use it internally. However, we include it here as an example of how your foundation might be able to formulate its own metric to compare otherwise incomparable outcomes. Of course, the downside of using internal metrics is that it means your cost-effectiveness analyses aren't interoperable with the work of others.

Income is one of the most common metrics for impact and has some major benefits. It is well understood, and easy to calculate and measure. However, there are many counterarguments, e.g., that income or GDP have been overly focused on and are easily gamed.[50] Income is most helpful when looking at multiple interventions that work on increasing long-term prosperity, and where hard data is available on income but not on softer metrics like subjective well-being.

As we have aimed to demonstrate in this chapter, there is no obvious winner in the debate about abstract impact metrics. Any of the four we've discussed could be a sensible choice for you, depending on the main types of costs and benefits you need to quantify and the types of CEAs you need to make comparisons with.

Use the chart below to consider pros and cons of using each of the options:

Metric	Strengths	Weaknesses
DALY	• Widely used (more results to compare with), including by the WHO and the World Bank • Captures many different types of ailments and risks • Already used in studies and research	• Doesn't capture non-health costs and benefits • Doesn't allow for comparison of benefits to humans and animals • Disability weights reflect uninformed judgments • Doesn't allow for states of being that are worse than death • Can't compare the outputs of analyses that use different age weights or time-discounting
QALY	• Widely used (more results to compare with), including by the USA and UK governments • Allows for states of being that are worse than death (theoretically)	Mostly per above, plus: • No standard methodology for determining disability weights
WELLBY	• Includes wider costs and benefits, outside of health (e.g., income, empowerment) • Based on self-reports of those with first-hand experience (vs. flawed, misinformed guesses) • Allows for states of being that are worse than death	• Doesn't allow for comparison of benefits to humans and animals • Few CEAs use them, so there are fewer analyses to compare with • Unclear where the neutral point is on the 1-10 scale, below which is worse than death (is it 2? 3? 5?) • Treats an improvement from 7 to 8 out of 10 as equal to from 2 to 3, which many find unintuitive

Welfare points	• Allow for cross-species comparison, including (theoretically) with humans • Allows for measurements of small changes (short-lived suffering in the order of days or months is often rounded to zero with other metrics) • Not many alternatives in the animal space	• Invented by Charity Entrepreneurship (few analyses to compare with; insufficient guidance on how to apply it consistently with CE) • Subjective components are based on the judgments of a small, unrepresentative group of people (CE staff) who disagree • Particularly abstract
Income	• Used in many economic analyses and educational impact evaluations • Is fairly concrete, despite being your 'abstract' metric • Can proxy things like enjoyment and freedom more than hard health metrics can	• Benefits to happiness/health do not scale linearly with income, and it's an open debate exactly how they do scale • Surveys suggest that income gains are less important to people than the health gains captured by other metrics

Common mistakes

Creating CEAs

Overcomplicating things: The more moving parts your CEA has, the greater the chances of making an error and the lower the chances of finding it. Don't shy away from accounting for complexity, but in most cases, a small number of variables and assumptions can get you about 90% of the way to the result that you'd get with the most thorough model possible.

Naive adjustments for conservatism:

• **Committing the 1% fallacy:** The 1% fallacy occurs when entrepreneurs pitch investors on a big, speculative idea, and then claim that even if they could only capture 1% of the market share or have a 1% probability of success, it would still be a good investment. Astute investors know not to fall for this pitch, because "to capture 1% of the market share" is an overly ambitious claim, and "1%" is often a lot less conservative or reasonable than it seems. Humans are not very good at accurately assessing small probabilities: 1% and 0.1% tend to be interpreted as the same small chance. Discounting and incorporating probabilities must be done separately for every assumption in your process, not just tacked on to the end of your analysis. If your intervention relies on 10 separate assumptions to be true, and each of those assumptions comes with a 50% discount, the cumulative discount is actually 0.098%, which is an order of magnitude less than 1%.

- **Taking worst-case scenarios:** When a CEA rests on several difficult-to-estimate quantities (e.g., the efficacy of an untested antidepressant, the number of crustaceans that exist, or the externalities of an unprecedented policy change), a common tactic is to model a worst-case scenario for these unknown values, so you can assume that the actual cost-effectiveness will be at least as good as the modeled result. For example, perhaps for each unknown value, you assume a number you feel about 95% confident will be less favorable than reality. This approach is less conservative than it seems! The more assumptions you add, the more hopelessly optimistic your so-called "worst-case scenario" becomes. If each of the five assumptions has a 95% chance of being right, that means your scenario has a 23% chance, roughly one out of four, of being too optimistic. That's hardly a worst case!

Double-counting impact: When an organization estimates the impact of its work, it generally takes total credit for the perceived impact of its work. On first glance, this looks perfectly reasonable. But this approach becomes problematic when other organizations also play a crucial role in achieving the impact. This can occur when two organizations do similar, synergistic work, like two advocacy groups that together achieved an important policy change. It can also occur with organizations that do different work towards the same goal: For example, if the Lead Exposure Elimination Project (LEEP) didn't exist, the governments of Malawi and Madagascar probably wouldn't have made progress on reducing lead levels in paint so quickly. But if Charity Entrepreneurship didn't exist, it probably would have taken LEEP longer to come into existence. And if it weren't for our funders, Charity Entrepreneurship couldn't operate. If all three of these groups model their counterfactual impact, you end up triple-counting one set of actual benefits in the world. Every organization has inflated cost-effectiveness analyses because it counts all the impact, but only a fraction of the total cost. Failing to account for all parties' participation can lead to strange outcomes, like lives saved in a location rather than the total population.

Assuming your impact continues indefinitely: As a rule, anything you build will eventually fall apart either due to failure, or the world changing and moving on. Just because an intervention got a farm to pledge to fortify its chicken feed now doesn't mean it will keep fortifying it for decades. Just because you passed a government policy change doesn't mean the policy won't be reversed in the future. On a similar note, it is often true that if you hadn't intervened, someone else might have eventually. So it's best to model your impact as speeding up the arrival of an intervention, and to model impacts for a limited time into the future.[51]

Incorrect assumptions about trends and distributions: Not every distribution is a normal distribution.[52] Many statistical techniques will go wrong if you assume something has a normal distribution when it doesn't. Trends that seem linear will often hit diminishing returns eventually. Trends that seem exponential will often turn out to be sigmoid (S-shaped) curves.

Interpreting CEAs

Taking CEAs literally: Cost-effectiveness analyses involve many judgment calls not only in philosophical matters regarding morality and epistemology, but also in much more arbitrary decisions about how to count or weigh things and which equation to use in a given scenario. In reading this, we hope you've developed more of an intuition for why you can't take expected value estimates literally (even when they're unbiased).

Comparing dissimilar CEAs: Because of all the semi-arbitrary decisions and subjective judgment calls involved in creating a CEA, the precise numbers you get are heavily contingent on who did the modeling. If you compare two completely different CEAs constructed under completely different methodologies, it's likely the differences in the final numbers are mostly a result of methodological artifacts, not real differences in the interventions' impact on the real world. To overcome this, you may need to adjust the CEAs so they can be compared on a level playing field.

Not catching the common mistakes in creating CEAs: Remember to look out for these common mistakes and avoid falling for poor reasoning.

Summary

- CEAs should play an important but limited role in grantmaking decision-making.

- The strengths of CEAs are (a) enabling direct comparison in terms of impact, (b) enabling formal sensitivity analysis, (c) transparency, and (d) score sensitivity.

- The weaknesses of CEAs are that they're (a) vulnerable and prone to single errors, (b) slow, (c) often heavily dependent on subjective value judgements, and (d) inefficient at capturing multiple effects and often neglect indirect effects.

- When it comes to output metrics, it's important to use both a concrete impact metric (e.g., lives saved) and an abstract one (e.g., DALYs or WELLBYs) to enable comparison between different types of interventions.

- There are trade-offs when deciding whether to review existing CEAs or create your own.

    - Costs of creating your own CEA:

        - Slower speed

        - Higher cost

        - Less access to information

    - Benefits of creating your own CEA:

        - Better incentives

        - Avoids adopting others' implicit assumptions

        - Contributes to greater diversity of perspectives

    - Best practices when vetting CEAs:

        - Check whether you agree with the assumptions

        - Conduct an evidence audit

        - Conduct a formula audit

        - Question whether the results hold up at scale

        - Make sure you know what is and isn't included, checking for missing costs (e.g., past or future costs; fundraising), missing indirect effects (e.g., on animals or the environment), and missing counterfactuals (e.g., opportunity cost of labor)

    - Best practices when improving CEAs:

        - Do your own thinking before looking at the model

        - Recreate the model in a new document

        - Focus on the most sensitive, least evidenced variables

- Model missing factors that may change the outcome

- Consider removing extraneous factors

- Common CEA mistakes to look out for:

  - Overcomplicating things

  - Naive adjustments for conservatism (like the 1% fallacy and "worst-case scenarios")

  - Double-counting impact

  - Assuming your impact continues indefinitely

  - Taking CEAs literally

  - Comparing dissimilar CEAs

Appendix D: Weighted-Factor Models

Role in your toolkit

If you were only allowed to carry one tool, the Swiss Army knife might be your choice. With multiple smaller tools attached, it can be useful in a large number of situations. But the knife pales in comparison to having a full toolkit from which to choose the right specialized tool for any given job.

The Swiss Army knife of decision-making is the **weighted-factor model** (WFM). It involves generating a set of criteria (often between three and 12) and assigning a weight to each. The options you're deciding between are then scored on each of the criteria. The final score incorporates the option's performance on, and the weighting of, each criterion, often by multiplying the two together.

WFMs are a useful tool for any decision with multiple important considerations. This includes both professional decisions, like what career to pursue or which projects to prioritize, as well as personal ones, like which city to live in. WFMs allow decision-makers to combine:

- Disparate types of evidence (e.g., both rational arguments and scientific papers about family-planning interventions)

- Objective and subjective factors (e.g., both the cost of living of a city and personal excitement about the lifestyle)

- "Hard" and "soft" quantitative inputs (e.g., cost-effectiveness given as "$/ life saved" or as a score out of ten).

Option	Total score	Addressable population	Modeled cost-effectiveness	Scientific evidence	Expert opinions
Weighting		20%	40%	25%	15%
Vaccine A	8.0	50M	$80/DALY	9	8
Vaccine B	6.6	36M	$100/DALY	7	6
Vaccine C	4.8	200M	$180/DALY	5	2
Vaccine D	4.4	1.2M	$300/DALY	10	6

As with a Swiss Army knife, some of the functionality of each tool is lost as we compress it to fit in one device. For weighted-factor models, what's lost is some of the detail and nuance on each factor that's included, as it's hard to capture all the nuance in a series of expert interviews when we're boiling it down to one or two numbers.

Grantmaking foundations are likely to use something like a WFM whenever we need to make a high-stakes choice between a number of options, like which interventions to prioritize, which grant applications to fund, or which candidate to hire. They serve as a summary of the information we have on each option, including the results of any cost-effectiveness analyses.

Strengths and weaknesses

Strengths

Systematic comparison: WFMs force us to compare options on the basis of a consistent set of criteria, which are given consistent importance. This makes for a more valid comparison between options than other tools, like cost-effectiveness analyses or consulting experts, which don't use a consistent structure or capture the exact same considerations across different options. When using other tools, it's easy to miss an important consideration when assessing an option, leading to an incomplete picture and an unfair comparison. WFMs make this impossible to miss, reducing the chance of gaps in our analysis. WFMs also force more equal application of rigor to each option, which makes for a fairer comparison.

Robust against errors and uncertainty in individual values: A large difference between CEAs and WFMs lies in the total weight that a single factor can hold. In a CEA, an outlier value for one variable can dominate the result, relative to many slightly above/below average numbers for other variables. For example, if an intervention could potentially affect a huge number of beings but has a very low chance of working, this initial huge number can still make all the other numbers in the CEA trivial. In contrast, one single large factor can affect a WFM far less, as each factor has a maximum weight. This means that there are limits to how much an error can throw off the result, or how much a single area we're uncertain about could determine the result.

Clear and efficient communication: WFMs efficiently communicate which factors went into a decision, their relative importance, and the performance of each option on those factors. This makes it easy to understand what led decision-makers to choose one option over another. Color-coding can be used to draw attention to areas of strength and weakness across multiple options and factors. Compare this with how long it would take to read a summary of expert interviews to understand the relative strengths of two options.

Builds in emphasis on convergence: Unlike CEAs, where individual outlier values can dictate the results, WFMs structurally favor options that look good according to a range of factors. This places emphasis on the convergence of evidence, which is important for making robust decisions.

Allows hard and soft inputs to be combined: Some important factors are easy to get a single hard number on (e.g., "total population affected by measles"); for others, it's impossible (e.g., "the tractability of founding a new charity in India"). In a WFM, both types of factor can be combined by converting hard inputs to soft ones, based on their z-scores.[53]

Weaknesses

Weighting of factors is arbitrary and subjective: There is no accepted methodology for how to arrive at the "correct" weightings of factors for a given decision.

Rationale behind scores is often opaque: In some cases, the number given for a factor is supposed to summarize a lot of different information (e.g., the strength of support for an intervention among 100 experts with very diverse viewpoints). This can make it hard to communicate why that score was given, especially when there will be some variance in the scores from different people.

Makes nonnumerical data look numerical: A concern with the WFM is that it assigns numerical ratings to nonnumerical data (e.g., the relative moral consideration given to different animals). This can confuse and mislead people as to the objectivity of the system if not explained clearly.

Hard to capture inconsistently important factors: The downside of the systematic nature of WFMs is that they don't naturally incorporate considerations that are very important for some options but completely irrelevant for others.

How to create a good WFM

There are eight steps for creating a good WFM:

1	Choose a benchmark
2	Generate a list of options
3	Choose factors (that are relevant, cross-applicable, and practical)
4	Pick tools for scoring each factor
5	Choose weightings
6	Determine any minimum thresholds
7	Score options (using iterative depth where appropriate)
8	Normalize inputs using z-scores (as needed)

Step 1: Choose a benchmark: When making a decision, it's helpful to compare each option to a baseline, or "do nothing" case, which can serve as a benchmark. For example, if you were creating a WFM comparing organizations to give a grant within the global health cause area, you might use GiveDirectly or the Against Malaria Foundation as your benchmark. If you were choosing what city to live in, the baseline would be the city you currently live in. If deciding who to hire, the baseline might be "no hire," or a previous staff member who just meets the acceptability bar.

Step 2: Generate a list of options: In some cases, there's a clear set of options (e.g., countries to start a charity in). In others, you'll need to come up with the list (e.g., career options or global health interventions). In the latter case:

- Try to generate at least twice as many options as are likely to be decent contenders.

- Get ideas from brainstorming, desktop research, or asking experts/advisors.

- Include a couple of options that you know are bad, to test out your model design and make it clear how good the best options are (e.g., for career options, you could include 'become the president').

Include your benchmark.

Step 3: Choose factors: Factors in the model can include anything from hard data, like CEA results, to very soft judgment calls, such as a general sense of logistical difficulty. Brainstorm more factors than needed and then narrow down based on the following criteria:

- **Relevance:** First and most obviously, the factor has to be relevant, i.e., it has to correlate with your endline goal. When determining which charity to fund, you might prefer some names of interventions above others, but a more relevant criterion would be how many studies have been conducted on each intervention.

- **Cross-applicability:** Tools must cross-apply. A column like "estimated lives saved from malaria" would work if you're only considering malaria interventions, but if you're considering many different global health interventions, it would only apply to some options. It's also important that columns differentiate between options. If a factor is scored as "medium" for all options, it does not add value to the decision-making process.

- **Practicality:** Can you get data on it? A column that would take 10 years to fill out is not helpful if you need to make a decision in a month. Is it more objective or subjective? Can others understand what the column indicates? These sorts of factors allow your model to be interpreted and criticized by outsiders.

- **Minimal overlap:** You want factors that are mutually exclusive to avoid double-counting certain considerations.

Finally, choose a set of five to 10 factors and group them by theme.

Output of Step 3 for a career-path WFM:

Theme	Short term impact			Long-term impact			Happiness	
Factor	CEA modelled	Outside view	Comparative advantage	Flexible skill building	Avoiding value drift	Learning what you're good at	Fun	Pay

Step 4: Pick tools for scoring each factor: Each factor must be scored by evidence (either a type of evidence or a specific source).

Step 5: Choose weightings: Start by ranking the themes in importance. Next, divide up 100% evenly between the themes and begin moving weight from less important themes to more important themes. Keep asking, "Does this make sense?" until you're happy with the weightings. Next, repeat this process for the factors within each theme. It's important to choose weights before starting to assess options and generating results; otherwise, you're more likely to tweak the weights after the fact so that the results better match your assumptions (i.e., using motivated reasoning).

Output of Steps 3-5 for a career path WFM:

Theme	Short term impact			Long-term impact			Happiness	
Importance	2			1			3	
Weight	35%			45%			20%	
Factor	CEA modelled	Outside view	Comparative advantage	Flexible skill building	Avoiding value drift	Learning what you're good at	Fun	Pay
Tool	CEA	Experts	Rationality	Experts	Rationality	Rationality	Rationality	Pay
Importance	1	3	2	1	2	3	1	2
Weight	15%	7.5%	12.5%	20%	15%	10%	15%	5%

Step 6: Determine any minimum thresholds: Think through whether any factors ought to have minimum thresholds below which an option is rejected. For example, there might be a minimum level of happiness, below which a career path is unsustainable.

In the context of grantmaking, you might have a minimum threshold on "transparency." For example, imagine you did a CEA for a charity that made it look really strong, but you spoke to others about the charity and learned it has a well-documented history of falsifying numbers and misleading donors. You'd likely give the organization a 1/10 on transparency and rightfully decide not to support them, no matter how strong the CEA or how well they performed on factors in the model.

You might also set a minimum threshold on the strength of evidence. CEAs aren't great at capturing significant differences in evidence, so many wise actors (including GiveWell) set a bar that the evidence needs to meet before treating an intervention as plausible. This could mean not funding an intervention without an RCT conducted on it, no matter how exciting it sounds in theory. The more skeptical you are, the higher this threshold for evidence would be.

Relative (instead of absolute) thresholds are also valuable, particularly when it comes to cost-effectiveness. For example, if GiveDirectly is a strong charity in almost every way but has low cost-effectiveness compared to many of the options you are considering, you might set a threshold to not evaluate in detail anything less cost-effective than GiveDirectly. This can be a way of using your grantmaking benchmark to save time assessing options.

Step 7: Begin scoring options: Next, it's time to use the pre-selected tools to score each option. For "soft" inputs (where we score from 1-10), you may wish to start by scoring the option you know the most about, or your benchmark option. You can then score other ideas in comparison to this. Once you've scored a column, you can sense-check the scores to see if their implied ranking of options by that score is sensible.

Output of Step 7 for a career path WFM:

Theme		Short term impact			Long-term impact			Happiness	
Factor	Total	CEA modelled (z-score)	Outside view (z-score)	Comparative advantage (z-score)	Flexible skill building (z-score)	Avoiding value drift (z-score)	Learning what you're good at (z-score)	Fun (z-score)	Pay (z-score)
Weight	100%	15%	7.5%	12.5%	20%	15%	10%	15%	5%
Option 1	0.33	-0.35	0.58	0.07	1.01	-0.05	0.20	1.34	-1.83
Option 2	0.14	1.12	-0.43	1.16	-1.14	-0.05	0.68	0.13	0.07
Option 3	0.17	-0.23	0.25	0.44	0.20	1.18	0.20	-0.27	-1.35
...	...	...	...	...	...	...	...	...	...
Option 15	0.09	-0.72	-1.44	0.80	0.74	-0.97	-1.72	1.34	3.54

When you have many options to score (e.g., you're vetting hundreds of grant applications), you may be able to save a lot of time by using the process of iterative depth. This involves assessing all options, using the fastest method first (heuristic evidence is particularly helpful) to rule out the least promising before vetting the remaining options with more rigor (e.g., assessing the scientific evidence). But be aware that ruling out options using one factor is only sensible if that factor is closely correlated with overall performance. Otherwise, you risk ruling out the best option simply because it performs poorly on one factor despite performing very well overall. This approach is also appropriate when vetting job applicants. First, assess all applicants on their performance on the application form, and then assess only those who pass a certain quality threshold.

Step 8: Normalize inputs using z-scores (as needed): Sometimes you'll be able to finish at Step 7, using the "sumproduct" formula in your spreadsheet software to calculate the weighted total scores for each option. But there are two common scenarios where you'll need to do some normalization first:

- **You have some "hard" inputs:** Whenever using hard inputs (e.g., population size) in a WFM, it's important to normalize these values. Otherwise, factors with big scores, like population size (expressed in millions), will dominate the total score when combined with subjective scores like tractability (scored between one and 10), or lower-magnitude hard inputs, like disease rate (expressed as a %).

- **When the "soft" scores for a factor don't reflect how significant the variance in performance actually is:** For example, if you're scoring a group of people on value alignment and you feel badly about giving anyone lower than six out of 10, you can use z-scores to reflect the fact that the difference between a six and a 10 is bigger than it may seem. On the other hand, if there's a factor where your scores are polarized but you think the actual difference in performance is less than this suggests, z-scores can help to narrow this.

The trick for normalizing these factors so that they can be combined is to use z-scores, a statistical measure of how many standard deviations a data point is away from the mean. In layperson's terms, the z-score is a measure of how much of an outlier a data point is. The closer to zero the z-score is, the less of an outlier (i.e., the more typical) it is.

For example, if a charity is considering rolling out an intervention in one of the five cities in the table below, the raw numbers do not clearly reveal which is more of an outlier: City B's high population or City D's high incidence of disease. By looking at their z-scores, we see the answer is City B (its population is 1.22 standard deviations from the mean). An example of the formula for calculating z-scores based on average and standard deviation is provided in the shaded cell:

	Population (mill)	Incidence of disease	Z-score (population)	Z-score (disease)
City A	1.8	76%	=(1.8-9.6)/7.3	0.19
City B	18.5	76%	1.22	0.19
City C	3.6	77%	-0.82	0.51
City D	15.6	78%	0.82	0.83
City E	8.5	70%	-0.15	-1.72

Average	9.6	75%
Standard dev.	7.3	3.2

Don't worry too much about the nitty-gritty. The point of this is that there is a helpful way to compare very different data sets using a standard unit. In our career path example, both modeled cost-effectiveness and salary are given in absolute values, so they will require normalization. **If any one factor requires normalization, you will need to normalize all factors so they can be combined**.

Output of Step 8 for a career path WFM:

Theme		Short term impact			Long-term impact			Happiness	
Factor	Total	CEA modelled (z-score)	Outside view (z-score)	Comparative advantage (z-score)	Flexible skill building (z-score)	Avoiding value drift (z-score)	Learning what you're good at (z-score)	Fun (z-score)	Pay (z-score)
Weight	100%	15%	7.5%	12.5%	20%	15%	10%	15%	5%
Option 1	0.33	-0.35	0.58	0.07	1.01	-0.05	0.20	1.34	-1.83
Option 2	0.14	1.12	-0.43	1.16	-1.14	-0.05	0.68	0.13	0.07
Option 3	0.17	-0.23	0.25	0.44	0.20	1.18	0.20	-0.27	-1.35
...	...	...	...	...	...	...	...	...	...
Option 15	0.09	-0.72	-1.44	0.80	0.74	-0.97	-1.72	1.34	3.54

Finally, you can use the weighted average z-score to determine which option looks the best (in this case, Option 1).

Using WFMs and CEAs together

Both these models are extremely useful when trying to assess impact. However, like all models, they don't perfectly reflect reality. As the saying goes, "All models are wrong, but some are useful." The key is to understand what each is good for and where each can mislead you, so they reliably improve the accuracy of your decision-making.

Because modeled cost-effectiveness is not the same as real cost-effectiveness, a CEA can look great despite an actual charity having low cost-effectiveness. Likewise, something can look great in all aspects of a WFM and fail to have an impact. Meanwhile, some great projects will be ruled out if only one of these models is used. That's why we strongly suggest using both types of models (and possibly others as well) to ensure more robust answers than you would get by leaning exclusively on one of them, or not using any formal modeling at all.

In our experience, it's more common for grantmaking decision-makers to rely on CEAs alone than on WFMs alone, so below we'll make a more thorough case for not relying entirely on CEAs.

The case for sandboxing

Sandboxing is when certain variables are confined to a metaphorical "sandbox" so as not to affect or dominate the entire model. This can mean bounding or otherwise limiting the strength of a certain variable. WFMs involve sandboxing because no single factor can cause one option to look best. An individual factor can rule options out, if you'd like, by using minimum thresholds (e.g., in a model of different career options, you might decide to rule out any option that scores below 3/10 on enjoyment). CEAs, in contrast, don't involve sandboxing in this way. If cost-effectiveness is calculated by multiplying three variables together, e.g., A x B x C, and if an option's value "A" is 1000x higher than other options, variable "A" will likely dominate the calculation.

1. Sandboxed models are more holistic and lower risk

The "deworming"[54] charities recommended by GiveWell score extremely well on models without sandboxing. They are very low-cost interventions, and the best available evidence suggests they improve beneficiaries' income many years later. When modeled in a CEA, even when discounted by over 90% for the low-quality evidence, they look unusually cost-effective.

GiveWell also recommends insecticide-treated bed nets for preventing malaria. According to GiveWell's CEAs, bed nets are not as cost-effective as deworming. However, when splitting the evidence out into different variables, bed nets look considerably stronger holistically; the evidence base is far stronger, with a wide-ranging set of studies with strong results across the board. The transparency is higher, and the mechanism by which they have an impact is better understood and more easily measurable (allowing for better ongoing monitoring). Mosquito nets also have more room to scale. These factors generally aren't captured in a CEA, but stand out clearly in a WFM. Other factors, like the quality of each charity's leadership and its organizational track record, can also be considered in the WFM. Going all-in on a low-evidence cost-effectiveness estimate is far riskier than sandboxing modeled cost-effectiveness and considering other factors in our decisions.

GiveWell is clear that its recommendations are not based on cost-effectiveness alone, and recently removed two deworming charities from its list of top charities, despite their highly modeled cost-effectiveness. Although these two models are useful, they can come to different conclusions and recommend different charities. Despite GiveWell being a highly numerical charity evaluator, it views CEAs as necessary but not sufficient for making final recommendations.

2. Sandboxed models are more robust to user error

Without sandboxing, models are vulnerable to being massively thrown off by user errors, and user errors are easy to make! For example, a simple error, such as dividing the population by the percentage of people affected, instead of multiplying it, can invalidate an entire CEA. For this reason, it's bad practice to rely entirely on models without sandboxing.

3. Massive differences between values that dominate CEAs are often less significant than they appear

One possible objection to sandboxing is that some options truly perform hundreds of times better on one variable than other options, and sometimes this should dominate the outcome. In this sense, sandboxing is not sufficiently "scope sensitive." Such examples most commonly arise with two factors: scale and cost-effectiveness. These can vary by 100x more easily than the quality of evidence or the leadership team can.

This is a clear case for making CEAs a part of our decision-making. However, we believe this point on scope sensitivity is overblown and is not a case against using sandboxing. This is a view shared by GiveWell, one of the most rigorous practitioners of the CEA. In the organization's words, "We often take approaches that effectively limit the weight carried by any one criterion, even though, in theory, strong enough performance on an important enough dimension ought to be able to offset any amount of weakness on other dimensions."[55] Let's walk through why a huge apparent difference in scale or cost-effectiveness might not be as important or large when carefully considered.

Scale: Scale is a factor that can swamp almost every other factor in a CEA, with order of magnitude differences common in both population and prevalence of an issue.[56] For example, Laos's population of around 8 million is more than 10 times smaller than neighboring Vietnam's approximate 100 million, and more than 100 times smaller than India's 1.4 billion. It's easy to see how differences like this can make India look like the best place to execute an intervention, even if we discount it by 75% for poor evidence. However, once we consider limiting factors, the relevant extent of this difference in scale may become far smaller. For example, India has 28 diverse states, so many interventions need to be implemented at the state level, while other countries would roll them out nationally. Perhaps it would be more sensible to model India by state, or focus on the most promising state? This one decision can change the population factor from 1.4 billion to 50 million (over 20x difference). Perhaps population isn't a limiting factor for the intervention, but funding or talent are. If so, the population might not even be relevant. If it's only possible to deliver 10 million treatments, any difference in the number of sick people beyond this is unimportant.

Cost-effectiveness: Sometimes a charity might look 1,000s of times more cost-effective than another, and this sometimes reflects reality. However, just as often, this apparent difference is the result of an oversimplified CEA model. Simple CEAs often exclude many costs (like those paid by other actors like governments, or incurred in the past or the future), naively over-estimate benefits (assuming, for example, the effect of an education intervention lasts forever), miss important indirect effects (such as on beneficiaries' families or communities, on animals, or on the environment), and ignore counterfactuals (as with assuming a problem would have lasted forever instead of being eventually solved without your intervention). In general, the more quality data acquired, the more these super-high cost-effectiveness estimates are lowered and brought in line with others.[57]

This is part of why both Charity Entrepreneurship and GiveWell have stopped trying to find the single most cost-effective option, and instead try to separate out "Tier A" options from lower tiers, knowing that these differences will be more robust than the difference between an outlier and other Tier A's.

Appropriately factoring CEAs into your assessments

Here's a useful analogy when thinking about how to factor CEAs into your assessments: If one Amazon product is rated 5/5 by three people, and another product is rated 4.6 by 3,000 people, which product would you buy? Most people would choose the 4.6, reasoning that three reviews are not very representative (and they could just be reviews from employees, friends, or paid reviewers. In fact, we might be more inclined to trust a lower rating with so few reviewers!). A weak CEA is like the 5-star review from three reviewers, while a GiveWell CEA is more like the 3,000-reviewer rating.

Using the Amazon analogy a bit differently, imagine three scenarios:

A. There is a product with a 1.8-star review from 10 reviewers

B. The product has a 1.8-star review from 1,000 reviewers

C. The product has a 3.8-star review from 1,000 reviews

Suppose a new review comes in from a friend of yours, giving the product 5 stars, with a bunch of photos and details explaining why the product is excellent. In Scenario A, your friend's glowing review will have a far more significant impact on your assessment of the product than in Scenario B. This is because your opinion will be less strongly held in A than in B.

Even when your initial opinions have been informed by the same amount of evidence, like in Scenarios B and C, and so are equally strongly held, your friend's review won't lead you to update your assessment to the same score. You would update your score closer to 5 stars in Scenario C than in Scenario B, because the new evidence is pointing towards a more surprising conclusion, and extraordinary claims require extraordinary evidence. It would take particularly strong evidence, like getting to try the product yourself, for you to update your score from 1.8 to close to 5 stars. Shifting our focus back to considering the results of a CEA on a charity, the above scenarios remind us that we should always keep in mind the strength of previous evidence on that charity and how surprising the CEA's results are in light of that evidence.

Let's apply this to the previous GiveWell example: GiveWell might have a prior opinion that it's difficult to affect income many years in the future with a minor health intervention such as deworming. So a CEA showing that deworming is amazing will need to be exceptionally strong to significantly change their assessment of deworming charities. A fairly uncertain CEA based on weaker evidence will not overly influence their prior opinion.

Getting the benefits of both models

If all types of models have significant flaws, and using no model is even worse, how can you make the best possible choice? The answer is similar to gathering information: layering one model on top of another makes up for gaps in each. A CEA might help to establish a broad area (say micronutrients) as highly effective, but you will have to take into account the strength of the team and many other factors when making the final call on a charity within that space. One way of bringing CEAs and WFMs together is to include the cost-effectiveness result as a factor in your WFM. This way, you can give the CEA significant weight (based on its strength) and can apply a minimum threshold to it (e.g., based on your benchmark), but you can also sandbox its impact on your ultimate decision.

Summary

- Weighted-factor models are useful for systematically comparing options, such as with interventions, grant proposals, experts, potential advisors, or candidates when hiring.

- The strengths of WFMs are (a) systematic comparison with equal application of rigor, (b) limiting the maximum damage caused by error or uncertainty in individual values, (c) clear and efficient communication, (d) building in an emphasis on convergence of evidence, and (e) allowing hard and soft inputs to be combined.

- The weaknesses of WFMs are (a) the weighting of factors is arbitrary and subjective, (b) the rationale behind scores is often opaque, (c) they make nonnumerical data look numerical, and (d) they have difficulty capturing factors that are very important for some options and irrelevant for others.

- WFMs involve sandboxing while CEAs do not. Using both avoids some of the risks of non-sandboxed models and allows you to use each type of model to compensate for the limitations of the other.

- The steps for creating a WFM are:

  1. Choose a benchmark.

  2. Generate a list of options.

  3. Choose factors (that are relevant, cross-applicable, and practical).

  4. Pick decision-making tools for scoring each factor.

  5. Choose weightings (by ranking factors in importance and then adjusting weightings accordingly).

  6. Determine any minimum thresholds (which may help eliminate options).

  7. Score the options (using iterative depth where appropriate).

  8. Normalize inputs using z-scores (as needed).

Appendix E: Spend-Down Rate

Every foundation has to consider the timeframe over which it'll spend down its pool funding. In some cases, there will be a practical ceiling on the spending rate (for example, it could be constrained by the rate at which assets can be liquidated), and in many cases, foundations will also set a floor on how fast to spend down, for legal reasons or personal reasons relating to the founder.

For private foundations, there is a legal minimum spend-down rate in many countries.[58] This is a base amount that needs to be granted year to year, and many countries also have overhead rules, e.g., if program staff are hired, their costs cannot be more than 10%–20% of total spending. The most widespread legal minimum is the 5% spend-down rate that applies to US private foundations. Canada has a similar rule, but for 3%, and the UK tends to be concerned if an organization's spending goes below 6% for a number of years. These requirements stipulate a minimum spend amount without considering the fact that the foundation's assets (which are typically invested) generally increase in value, sometimes by more than is spent each year. This allows foundations, if they choose, to exist in perpetuity; some of the largest foundations have far outlived their founders. Hitting this legal minimum and existing in perpetuity was a fairly common foundation strategy historically, but is less common with newer foundations. The Rockefeller Foundation is an example of a foundation that uses this minimal spend-down approach.

A large number of foundations aim to spend down their funding within a predetermined timeframe, such as within the founders' lifetime. This system makes a lot of sense if the founders want to be highly involved in the foundation's activities. The Gates Foundation is an example of a foundation that uses the time-based approach, with a requirement that the endowment be fully deployed within 20 years of the end of the founders' lives.

But beyond these constraints, a debate rages between those who believe that foundations should aim to deploy all their funding as quickly as possible, those who believe they should invest their principal to spend in the future, and a spectrum of opinions in between. This debate hinges on three questions:

1. Will spending a dollar yield higher marginal cost-effectiveness now or in the future?

2. Will you be able to spend more money now or in the future?

3. Will the indirect effects be better from spending now or later?

These are empirical questions that are, in principle, answerable (just not easily). We can't explore their full depth in one short appendix, but we can lay out the key considerations and explain why we lean towards spending earlier rather than later.

When will your marginal cost-effectiveness be higher?

Given the option of giving a dollar now vs. giving a dollar later, you should decide based on when you have the better marginal impact per dollar. That depends on the availability of cost-effective interventions vs. the availability of funding for those interventions, and on your ability to make good decisions about which problems are important and which interventions are most cost-effective.

Availability of cost-effective interventions

Will the world have more room for improvement at a low cost in the future than it does today? In other words, will the marginal cost-effectiveness curve be "lower" and "wider" in the future?

Marginal cost-effectiveness curve

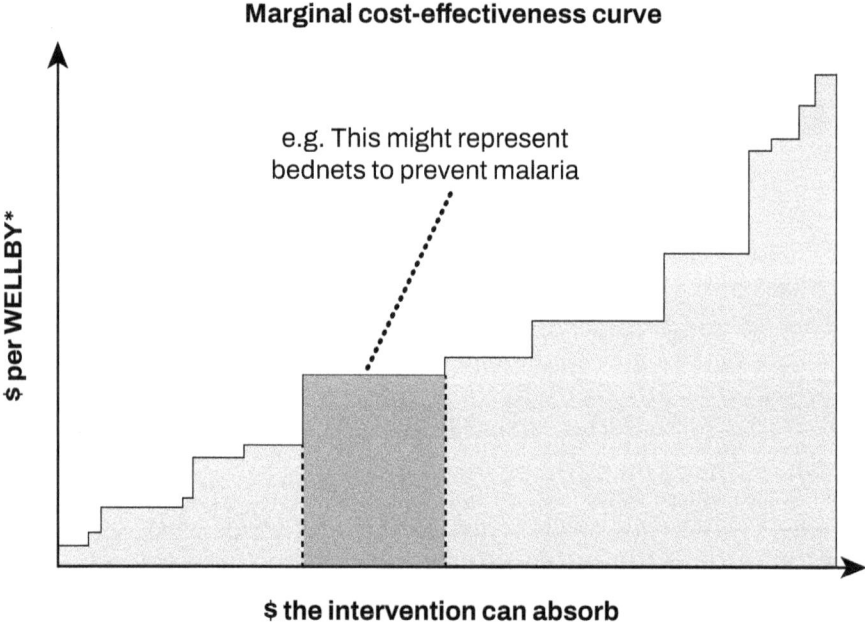

e.g. This might represent bednets to prevent malaria

$ the intervention can absorb

* This type of curve applies to any impact metric – WELLBYs used for illustrative purposes

The answer depends on a number of factors:

1. Progress improving the world: If humanity successfully deploys resources today to fix problems, then today's "low-hanging fruit" will already have been picked in the future (i.e., the leftmost opportunities on the cost curve will already have been taken). One clear example of this is that extreme poverty is trending downwards globally.[59] This pushes us towards spending now. That said, it's possible that new problems will arise in the future, meaning there are lower-cost opportunities available to have an impact. However, it will often be cheaper still to prevent those new problems from arising in the first place.

2. **When we have more "leverage" over the future:** In many cases, it will be cheaper to prevent a problem from emerging or stop it before it gets out of hand than waiting to address it later. We have a unique opportunity today to spend our resources in this kind of preventative fashion. For example, it may be highly cost-effective to prevent factory farming in countries where animals are still farmed more traditionally. However, it will also be too early to mitigate many future problems, because we're often clueless about the consequences our current actions will have far into the future. As such, the direction this factor pushes us in will depend on the case at hand.

3. **Technological progress:** Future technology will make it possible to solve problems in ways that aren't available today, in some cases at far lower costs. For example, new vaccines or gene-driven technology may make it far cheaper to prevent certain diseases, like malaria. This will create new interventions on the left of the cost curve and push down the cost of existing interventions.

4. **Intervention discovery:** The interventions that we have for tackling a given problem are the product of the technology available and the ideas we've come up with for using that technology. Evidence-based philanthropy is still early in its lifecycle, so even holding technology constant, there is a lot of progress to be expected in discovering new cost-effective interventions on the left side of the cost curve. For example, progress in understanding mental health could help us use existing technology to improve it far more cost-effectively.

5. **Execution capabilities within the nonprofit sector:** We're not only early in our collective journey of discovering cost-effective interventions; we're also early in our journey of building expertise in executing those interventions as efficiently as possible. Independent of the factors above, we should expect the cost of each step in the cost curve to come down over time. For example, effectiveness-focused charities have only recently been launched to advocate specific health policies. Over time, these will accumulate learnings about which tactics are most effective, and how to operate efficiently. And, in case it wasn't hard enough to figure out how these factors play out in general, we must consider how these factors play out differently for different cause areas.

Supply of funding for those interventions

Will the world have more available funding targeted at the most cost-effective interventions in the future? The greater the available pool of funding, the lower the marginal impact of your donations (see the figure below: "willingness to donate" captures both the amount of philanthropic funding available and the fact that effectiveness-focused funders have benchmarks of cost-effectiveness below which they will not spend).

Marginal cost-effectiveness curve meets funding supply curve

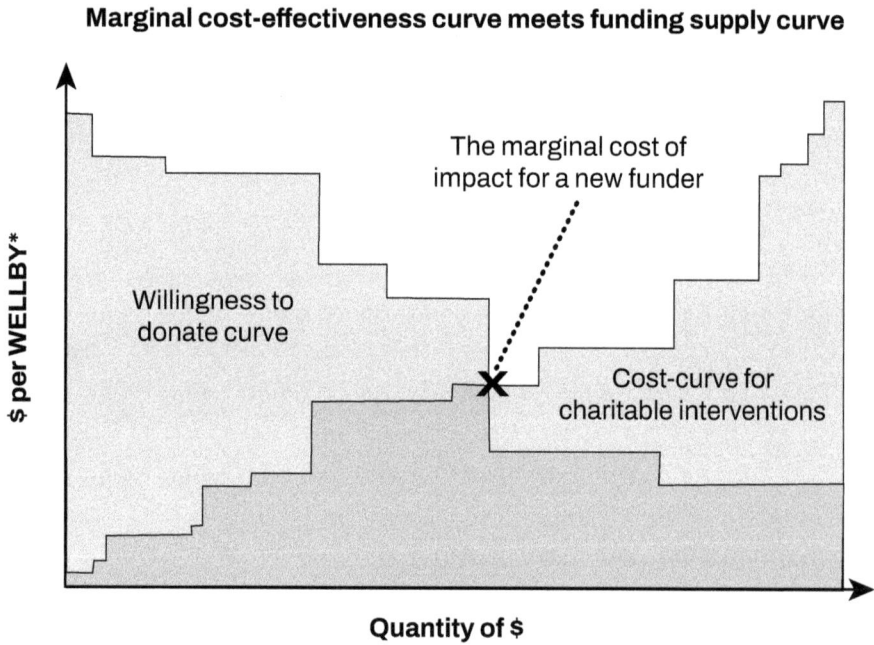

This future state of this funding supply curve depends on the **growth of effectiveness-focused donations**: In the future, do we expect philanthropic donations to grow? There is good evidence suggesting that total donations are correlated both with GDP and inequality;[60] the former has trended upwards for most of human history[61] while the latter is more variable but has trended upwards in many of the countries that donate the most (like the U.S. and U.K.) over the past 50 years.[62] There is also the possible impact of any moral progress on the number and generosity of donors. Based on these factors, we'd bet on total donations growing in the future.

But the average amount of consideration given to the cost-effectiveness of donations is pretty low in most cause areas. Only the proportion of total donations going towards the most cost-effective interventions is relevant for the "spend now vs. later" debate. Do we expect this proportion to grow over time? There are reasons to believe it will, such as progress made in the global health and development cause area. But this is hardly a sure thing, as there are other philanthropic trends that focus less on cost-effectiveness and more on other values like justice, participation, or sustainability.

It's difficult to reach a robust conclusion on the likely trajectory of the funding supply curve. Among the funders we've spoken to, the prevailing belief is that funding will expand, which pushes us towards spending now vs. later.

Your ability to make good grantmaking decisions

Will you be able to make better grantmaking decisions now or in the future? This depends on:

1. Ethical progress: Will humanity get better at ethics, leading to better decisions about which problems are important to solve?

2. Epistemological progress: Will humanity develop better methods for deciding what is cost-effective, or reach better conclusions about which of the methods already available to us are best?

3. Scientific progress: Will humanity improve the size and quality of the empirical evidence base for deciding what is and isn't cost-effective?

4. Personal grantmaking progress: Will you become better as an individual at making decisions, either when grantmaking or leading a grantmaking organization?

These considerations broadly point towards us making better grantmaking decisions in the future. However, the best way to make personal progress on grantmaking is through practice, so we advise beginning to make grants as soon as possible.

When will you be able to spend more?

Having laid out the factors that determine whether you can spend a dollar more cost-effectively today or in the future, the next question is: When will you be able to donate the most dollars? Typically, the backbone of the belief that we should "be patient" and donate later is the notion that by investing the money today, you will end up donating more in the future. But this is not as clear as it may seem at first.

Return on investment, adjusted for inflation

It is fairly uncontroversial that on a long-enough timeline, barring any societal collapse, investments will earn a return that exceeds inflation. While the S&P 500 has had an inflation-adjusted annualized return of ~7% since its inception in 1926, not all markets have fared so well, and some have completely ceased to exist. Credit Suisse recently attempted to adjust the global equity returns figure to take selection bias into consideration and concluded that there was an annualized real return of ~5% from 1900 to 2019.[63] At this rate of growth, an invested pool of funding doubles every 14 years.

But before tallying this as a win for the case for spending later, it's worth digging a bit deeper than a simple base rate. Do you expect that the period of time you might postpone giving for (e.g., the next 20 years) will match this base rate? Or do you have reason to believe that the risk of investment collapse or hyperinflation is unusually high?

Willingness and ability to donate

You know that you're willing to donate significant funds to improve the world today, that you have the good health to work on deploying the funding, and/ or the ability to attract talented people to deploy it for you. But the future is less certain. People's values change over time (and not always for the better), health can take unexpected turns, and organizations can find themselves unable to attract talent the way they once could. In our experience, people structurally underestimate the size of this risk. Taking all these factors into consideration usually leads to a significantly lower growth rate in forecast future donations, and may even lead one to expect future donations to be lower than they are today.

A common rebuttal to this point is that you can simply put your money into a fund that is legally compelled to disburse funds to the charitable sector. This is good practice, but there is a huge difference between giving and giving effectively. One can propose tactics to mitigate the risk that your future self is less motivated by effectiveness than your current self; for example, you could design the fund such that its decisions must be approved by a board, but this board is made up of people who are equally vulnerable to value drift. We're yet to see a surefire solution to this problem.

In addition to the risk that you are no longer willing to give, there is the risk that you may no longer be able to. You could lose control over your fortune, for example. There is also the special case of existential risks. If some threat like a large-scale nuclear war, a human-made pathogen, or an asteroid ends humanity, it will be too late to spend our resources to improve the world. The non-zero chance of such an outcome should lead you to discount your estimates of how much you can donate in the future by investing to give.

When are the indirect effects of spending better?

So far, we have discussed the considerations that determine whether you will have a higher direct impact through donations now or in the future. But there are significant indirect effects to consider as well.

Norm-setting and effects on reputation

Deciding to spend later normalizes this decision within the philanthropic sector. You may think this is a good thing because you think the facts indicate that more philanthropists should take this path. However, even if it *is* the right path for you, that is likely not the case for many other philanthropists. It is human nature to want to keep our money for ourselves, and even someone who has made the decision to give it away will have some hesitancy about it at the back of their mind. When a philanthropist decides to give later, it leaves the option open for not giving at all, and this is what makes giving later so enticing. This is usually entirely subconscious, which is why it is so dangerous for giving later to become the norm. Those who are most receptive to arguments advocating giving later are usually those most at risk of changing their minds and not giving as much, or at all, later down the line.

On the other hand, when individuals publicly and rapidly donate large amounts of their worth to effective causes, it may encourage other wealthy individuals to give, give more effectively, and give larger proportions of their wealth.

Opportunity cost of grantmaking talent

The longer you take to deploy a certain pool of philanthropic funding, the longer you occupy talented people who would otherwise be doing valuable work. The amount of labor you use for grantmaking is proportional to how much you spend, so spending more slowly does mean using less labor, but it is not a linear relationship, and there is a minimum amount of labor required to keep the lights on at a foundation.

Impact on your foundation's organizational culture

Aggressive spend-down aspirations can contribute to a higher general sense of urgency in the foundation. They also tend to encourage shorter feedback loops, higher levels of risk tolerance, and bigger bets. Depending on the type of culture you would like to promote in your organization, this could increase or decrease the attractiveness of a rapid spend-down.

Second-order benefits compound over time

In the same way that financial investments today can yield future returns, so can investments in impact today. For example, curing a person of blindness today allows them to use their improved health to earn more money earlier in their lives than they otherwise would, or to make further investments into their health, such as through exercise. Their children may grow up happier, and so on. Or, as another example, recipients of cash transfers might use them to replace thatched roofs with metal ones, or kerosene lamps with solar-powered ones, generating cost savings that represent a far higher return on investment than you could expect to earn on financial investments.[64] It's unsurprising that people who have the most basic problems could achieve a higher return by spending their money on simple solutions than they could by investing it.

All three of these other considerations point towards spending sooner rather than later.

In summary, the decision between spending now vs. later is not an easy one. We do not have conclusive evidence in one direction or the other. However, our assessment of the factors above leads us to lean towards most foundations giving sooner rather than later. We also believe that whether you plan to do most of your giving now or in the future, practice is key. As such, we recommend that you begin your grantmaking journey as soon as possible. Start with smaller "learning grants" and then ramp up your spending over time according to your strategy on giving now vs. later.

Appendix F: Guide to Starting a Funding Circle

Purpose of a funding circle

Funding circles represent a simple yet powerful way to improve donor coordination across cause areas. This is a brief guide to why funding circles are needed, what constitutes a good funding circle, and how to start one.

What does an ideal funding structure look like?

The funding structures in most cause areas leave plenty of room for improvement. Funders don't tend to have a deep awareness of each other, information sharing is limited, and great organizations often fall through the cracks.

A far more ideal structure would be one with a clear pathway for organizations to scale up, moving from smaller funders to larger ones. A diverse range of informed funders would share notes and information with each other. This would enable them to notice gaps between them and avoid missed opportunities. Shared information and perspective would mean their scopes would overlap somewhat, so that high-impact organizations in their cause area would always get the necessary funding.

The for-profit sector often does a better job of this with clear seed; series A, B, and C rounds, and coordinated investment rounds. Although structures like this are less common in nonprofits, there are some established systems that can reliably increase donor coordination and thus impact. One structure that does these things well is a funding circle. Funding circles can address these challenges and make philanthropy significantly more effective in a few key ways:

1. They provide a centralized point of contact for grant seekers, simplifying the application process.

2. They facilitate information-sharing among funders, leading to more informed decision-making.

3. They help ensure comprehensive coverage of a cause area, reducing gaps and overlaps in funding.

4. They streamline the funding process, benefiting both grantors and grantees.

Key components of a funding circle

Establishing a funding circle requires a few essential elements, within which there is a lot of room for variation:

Membership criteria

To build a funding circle, you need a methodology for identifying the right individuals with whom to coordinate. The most productive conversations come from funders who support similar areas or share similar methodologies. There can also be clearer and logistical requirements, such as:

• Demonstrated commitment to the specific cause area

• Minimum annual donation amount to a given area

• Total annual philanthropic contributions

• Recommendation from existing members

- Relevant expertise or experience in the field

The highest temptation with membership is to allow in far too many actors or far too few: a funding circle with two people can lead to very high levels of coordination, but you are likely letting a lot of folks fall by the wayside. On the other hand, a collaboration of 200 will only be able to coordinate in a fairly shallow way. The purpose of the circle will largely determine the best number of members to facilitate that purpose.

If you are unsure about numbers, we have found a sweet spot in the seven to 14 core members range (with room to include more members in an "outer circle"; see below). This provides sufficient diversity of views and actors to benefit from coordination, while also encouraging co-granting among them. This is also a feasible number to have the bulk of people actively participate in a single call or meeting.

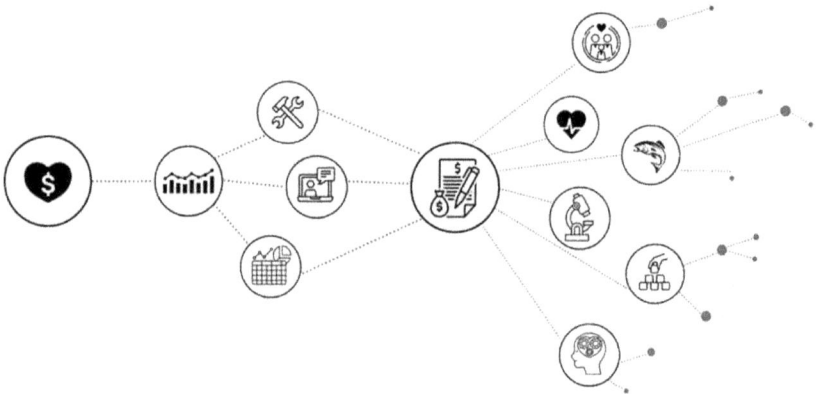

The circle's grantmaking process

The grantmaking process you want to run together and the level of coordination that process requires will play a major role in shaping your funding circle. Some key strategic decisions in this area include:

- Open vs. closed application rounds
- Which application process stages are shared between members
- Shared due diligence
- Communal resources (for example, shared funding or staff)
- How often you meet or otherwise communicate about the opportunities

For example, a circle's grantmaking process could look like the following, including three conversations throughout the round for funders to discuss and coordinate with each other:

1. An open application round twice a year, asking all applicants the same questions

2. Shared initial screening done by two designated circle members

3. Separate in-depth reviews by each funder, picking their own charities for deep dives

4. Final decision-making and funding allocation, with each funder making their own final calls

---

Common question: When should you hire staff for a funding circle?

The three main factors that lean people towards having staff operating or coordinating the funding circle are 1) the amount of money moved through the circle, 2) available hours of the foundations participating in the circle, and 3) how time-intensive the granting process is.

For example, if you have eight members each working a full-time job, but donating seven-figure sums in their spare time, having a higher-coordination circle with a full-time staff would be well worthwhile. On the other hand, if the total needed amount of work is less than 10 hours a week or can be easily absorbed by a few of the members who have full-time staff, getting a staff member to coordinate might not be worth the hassle of hiring.

Examples from the field: funding circles in action

Funding circles operate on a spectrum of coordination levels. Neither the higher- nor lower-coordination circles are inherently better, but both serve different purposes and member preferences. Thus, it is common for someone to be a member of both a smaller, higher-coordination group and a larger, lower-coordination group. Below are some real-world examples of circles taking different approaches. There are far more funding circles beyond these, but we have either directly been a member of these or have heard positive things from more than three of their members.

Lower coordination examples

Senterra Funders (Senterra)[65]

Senterra is a network of funders dedicated to ending factory farming. Members range from those donating $250,000 annually to those contributing over $20 million. The group employs a small staff to assist with research, vetting opportunities, and general coordination. This structure helps reduce the risk of duplicate funding and helps identify promising opportunities that might otherwise be overlooked.

Big Bang Philanthropy[66]

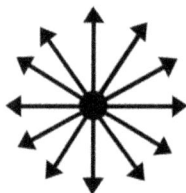

This group focuses on global health and development. Big Bang Philanthropy has an interesting approach: if an organization receives support from five or more Big Bang members, it becomes a "Big Bang charity." New members of the network are expected to provide significant support to at least five of these designated charities, but there is no formalized shared pipeline.

Mid-level coordination examples

Agency Fund[67]

The Agency Fund represents a step up in coordination, focusing on improving human agency. While some members operate fairly independently, they do have a shared application pipeline, and some members even pool their funding, which is then directed by the staff of the Agency Fund itself.

Charity Entrepreneurship Seed Network[68]

This network provides initial seed funding to charities graduating from the Charity Entrepreneurship incubation program.[69] The deal-flow pipeline is entirely shared, as is the applicant information that members receive. They conduct two rounds per year, featuring five to eight charities per round, and then decide which of these they want to fund. Coordination includes a couple of calls and events annually, but donor-to-donor coordination remains relatively minimal, and final decisions are independently made.

Higher coordination examples

AIM Mental Health Funding Circle[70]	
	The AIM Mental Health Funding Circle operates with a high level of coordination. It maintains a shared pipeline of opportunities, but without pooled funding: each funder independently decides what they consider to be most impactful to support. The circle holds regular conversations and meetings. A unique feature is the streamlined due diligence process, through which often a single funder (typically the one providing the most funding to a particular opportunity) takes the lead on vetting.

Strategic Animal Funding Circle[71]	
	The AIM Strategic Animal Funding Circle is a small group with a focus on smaller and newer animal organizations. The circle has regular open rounds with high levels of overlap in due diligence, and members focus on neglected areas within the animal space (small farmed animals, farmed animals in LMICs). If FAF were a conference, this circle might be closer to a dinner party.

Most of these circles are open to new members and can be worth joining if they fit your philanthropic focus areas. But they all have many shared characteristics and lessons that can also be cross-applied to other cause areas and circles.

Starting your own funding circle

If you're a funder looking to initiate a funding circle, the basic process consists of the following steps:

1. Connect with like-minded funders through events, networks, or professional circles.

2. Establish a core group, ideally with two organizers and about five funders.

3. Define your circle's focus and desired level of coordination.

4. Create a basic structure for meetings and communication.

5. Set up an application process or deal flow system.

Remember, you can start small. One person with time and two more people with funding can be enough to get the process going, although we've found it's often easier to start with two people dedicating time and about five people providing funding.

When thinking of starting a new funding circle, it's often worth reaching out to funding circles in adjacent spaces in case they can fit your needs, like the ones above, or have members who might also want to join yours.

A default structure for funding circles

While each circle may have its own operating style, here's a basic structure that we have found to work well:

- Five to 10 core funders per circle, plus a larger "outer circle" of two to 10 funders who receive emails about promising potential grantees, but don't actively participate.

- Two collaborative open-application grant rounds per year, each about two months.

- Each funder makes independent funding decisions after discussing opportunities with others in the circle.

- The process for each round could look something like this:

  1. Circle members send out a Request for Proposals (RFP) to relevant networks. Allow one month from RFP to application deadline.

  2. After the deadline, narrow down applications to the 15-30 most promising.

  3. Chairs send screened applications to circle members for review. Allow five to seven days for review.

  4. First Zoom call: Members discuss applications and assign "point persons" for further due diligence on promising candidates.

  5. Second Zoom call (two to three weeks later): Members share due diligence findings and new insights.

  6. Third Zoom call (two to three weeks later): Members announce their respective decisions. Chairs promote collaboration and consider efficient donation swaps to save on fees.

Tips for running a great funding circle

Based on our experience running five funding circles in various areas, here are some cross-applicable lessons:

What works well

1. Regranting with experts: Some circle members have given re-granting funding to cause area experts who then participate as members. These tend to be both deeply informed and engaged re-granters, allowing for deeper and more informed conversations.

2. Light and heavy members: Have five to 12 dedicated core members but maintain a larger mailing list with a lower bar for involvement. This allows you to share great opportunities more widely. In our experience, the larger network typically contributes around 10-20% of total funding.

3. Focusing on quality: This means people who will have productive conversations. It's okay to remove members who don't fit well, even if they donate significantly.

4. Open rounds: These are crucial for bringing in new grantees and avoiding funding the same organizations every year. Funding circles can handle the workload of open rounds more efficiently than individual funders.

5. Narrow scopes: Keeping the circle's focus relatively narrow allows for alignment among funders, higher-quality conversations, and manageable application numbers.

6. Consistent communication: Choose a communication medium (Slack, email, monthly meetings, etc.) and stick to it to prevent losing touch.

What hasn't worked well

1. Mismatched members: A few ill-fitting members can significantly worsen the experience for everyone. This could be caused by personality conflicts or vast differences in funding amounts. Regardless, the quality of interaction is more important than the sheer quantity of members. Many struggling funding circles have become too large or diverse in viewpoints. It is better to start small with aligned members who trust each other's recommendations.

2. Overly broad focus: Resist the temptation to cover more ground than you realistically will. It's easier to increase your scope later than to reduce it. Start narrow with the topic and people, expand later.

3. Unbalanced membership: Avoid situations where one member contributes over 50% of total grantmaking.

4. Inconsistent transparency preferences: Differing practices regarding public transparency about recipients and explanations for grants can look confusing.

Areas with mixed or unclear results

1. Monthly meetings between rounds: These can promote a sense of community and aid coordination, but often suffer from low attendance due to busy schedules.

2. Standardized grantee reporting: Usage and associated results have been inconsistent in our experience.

3. For-profit grantees: Including these can lead to unique due diligence challenges, as well as some difficulty comparing opportunity promisingness, but can open up new opportunities.

4. Institutional members: The effectiveness of including these is still unclear. There are benefits to having more members, but institutions typically coordinate in quite different ways than private foundations do.

Appendix G: Cause-Area Deep Dives

Global health

What is this cause area?

Global health focuses on improving health outcomes in LIMC through cost-effective interventions that tackle preventable diseases and health inequities. The field spans everything from direct services (like vaccination campaigns or mosquito-net distribution) to health-system strengthening. Unlike healthcare in wealthy nations, global health work often addresses basic needs with interventions that can save lives at remarkably low cost, sometimes just a few thousand dollars per life saved.

The moral case is pretty straightforward: preventable suffering should be addressed regardless of where it happens. And because costs are dramatically lower in lower-income settings, donors can often achieve far more impact per dollar. This is probably one of the few cause areas that looks great across a huge number of moral worldviews; no one thinks it's okay for children to die of easily preventable diseases.

Example of a possible benchmark charity

GiveWell's rigorous evaluations have identified several standout organizations in this space. The Malaria Consortium's seasonal malaria chemoprevention program gives preventive medication to kids under five during peak malaria season. This and other programs have strong evidence of effectiveness, great cost-efficiency, good transparency, and the ability to make good use of more funding. Their interventions are based on solid science, careful implementation, and tight monitoring to make sure real-world impact happens. They're also big enough to absorb tens of millions of dollars a year.

With $1 million invested in global health, you can save around 300 lives through cost-effective programs like distributing insecticide-treated bednets in malaria-endemic regions.

Other funders in this area

This space includes a wide range of funders. The Gates Foundation is the biggest private player, investing billions of dollars. Others include Coefficient Giving, the Mulago Foundation, and the Big Bang Philanthropy coalition. On the public-private side, big multilateral organizations like the Global Fund (AIDS, TB, Malaria) and Gavi (vaccines) pool funding from governments and donors. There are also lots of individual donors giving through platforms like GiveWell, EA Funds, and the Life You Can Save.

The biggest weakness of the area

Global health's primary weakness is its middling level of neglect. While it's still dramatically underfunded compared to health spending in wealthy countries, it does attract significant attention. Philanthropy and governments together contribute tens of billions to international health assistance. This relative crowdedness means that for donors specifically seeking the absolute highest-leverage opportunities, even more neglected areas might offer greater marginal returns, though usually at the trade-off of having less robust evidence behind them.

Income and livelihoods

What is this cause area?

Income and livelihoods programming aims to increase economic well-being for people in poverty through interventions that boost earning potential and financial stability. This is a broad cause area that includes cash transfers, vocational training, agricultural support, education initiatives, and entrepreneurship development. The theory of change is straightforward: economic improvements help people meet basic needs, gain agency, and build resilience against shocks. Unlike programs that provide specific goods or services, many income-focused interventions empower recipients to decide for themselves how to allocate resources. Evidence suggests that income increases can lead to better nutrition, health, education, and overall well-being, potentially creating sustainable paths out of poverty.

Example of a possible benchmark charity

Pratham runs evidence-based education programs that improve learning outcomes in India, including its Teaching at the Right Level approach, which significantly improves literacy and numeracy skills. One Acre Fund supports smallholder farmers with financing, farm inputs, agricultural training, and market access. For $1 million, One Acre Fund can serve approximately 5,000 farming families, increasing annual farm income by roughly $100 per household, which is a 40-50% increase for many participants. This translates to around 25,000 people impacted. Similarly, $1 million invested in Pratham can deliver educational interventions to roughly 100,000 children, improving their future earning potential.

Other funders in this area

The livelihoods space includes a mix of funders. The Livelihoods Impact Fund brings in corporate investors like Danone and Mars to finance sustainability projects that support smallholder farmers. The Mastercard Foundation focuses on education and youth livelihoods primarily in Africa. Traditional philanthropic players include the Ford Foundation, Rockefeller Foundation, and IKEA Foundation. Major multilateral funders like the World Bank and USAID deploy billions in livelihoods programming. The space also includes impact investors aiming for both social and financial returns through social enterprises that create jobs or reach underserved communities.

The biggest weakness of the area

One of the biggest weaknesses is mixed prioritization by beneficiary communities themselves. Research from IDinsight shows that when people are asked what they'd prefer, they often rank health interventions above income-focused programs per dollar spent. This raises a tough question: Should funders prioritize income generation when many beneficiaries might prefer immediate support for their health?

The area also faces impact measurement challenges. Some programs show modest or inconsistent effects, and success can depend heavily on context; what works in one region may not work in another. This makes it harder to scale successful models widely.

Policy-focused economic growth

What is this cause area?

Policy-focused economic growth aims to tackle systemic barriers that hold back development. The idea is to change rules and regulations that block economic progress. This means things like restrictive immigration policies, excessive land-use rules, or trade barriers. The theory is simple but powerful: some policy changes can unlock massive value by removing artificial constraints on productive activity. The big appeal here is leverage. A single policy shift can affect millions and create economic value far beyond the cost of the advocacy it took to get there.

Example of a possible benchmark charity

The Copenhagen Consensus Center is known for its rigorous economic analysis of policy options, ranking interventions by their benefit-cost ratios and influencing government priorities in multiple countries. The Foundation for Economic Development (FED) advocates evidence-based economic policies promoting growth, focusing on regulatory reform, trade liberalization, and innovation policy. For approximately $1 million invested in these organizations, donors can fund comprehensive research and advocacy campaigns that influence billions in government spending. Copenhagen Consensus estimates that every dollar spent on their research influences approximately $1,000 in more effective government spending. Similarly, FED's work on immigration and zoning reform has helped shape policies with potential economic benefits measured in the billions annually.

Other funders in this area

This space has a fairly unique funding landscape. Big funders include the William and Flora Hewlett Foundation (which backs evidence-driven economic policy), the Arnold Foundation (focused on research-based reform), and the Omidyar Network (which supports market-oriented approaches). The World Bank also plays a major role here, using both research and conditional lending to push for policy reform. Occasionally, corporate foundations get involved too, especially around issues like trade or regulatory efficiency. Still, total philanthropic funding in this space remains relatively small, especially compared to other development approaches.

The biggest weakness of the area

The biggest challenge is finding strong, effective organizations working in this space. The evidence base can also be mixed and politically charged. Experts often disagree about the true effects of specific policies, like changes to the minimum wage or tax structures, and it's hard to rigorously attribute economic outcomes to individual reforms. Impact evaluation is tricky. And because economic policy is often ideologically divisive, it can be tough to build bipartisan support, which introduces reputational risks for funders. On top of that, policy requires long-time horizons, and the odds of success can be low. Many campaigns fail due to political dynamics beyond anyone's control.

X-risk/AI

What is this cause area?

AI safety and existential risk focus on reducing catastrophic threats from advanced artificial intelligence systems. The field addresses concerns that increasingly powerful AI might become unaligned with human values, potentially threatening humanity's future. The field spans technical research on how to keep AI systems safe and controllable, governance work on responsible development policies, and forecasting efforts to anticipate potential risks. The underlying premise is that we're in a critical window: alignment and governance problems must be solved before we reach transformative AI systems that could surpass human capabilities.

Example of a possible benchmark charity

Redwood Research and Epoch are standout organizations addressing AI safety challenges from complementary angles. Redwood Research conducts applied technical research on controlling advanced AI systems, focusing on practical alignment experiments and developing interpretability tools to better understand neural networks. Epoch specializes in AI forecasting and strategy research, tracking progress in AI capabilities and analyzing potential development trajectories. For around $1 million, donors can fund three to four technical research projects or support a four-person research team for a year, potentially developing safety techniques that shape how major AI labs build in safeguards.

Other funders in this area

The AI safety funding landscape has evolved rapidly in recent years. Coefficient Giving is the largest philanthropic funder, having committed hundreds of millions to AI safety research and governance. The Survival and Flourishing Fund uses donor lotteries to distribute grants to various AI safety initiatives. Some traditional foundations like Sloan and MacArthur have made smaller investments in AI governance. Recently, major AI companies, including Microsoft, Google DeepMind, and Anthropic, have established their own safety teams and now also provide some external research funding.

The biggest weakness of the area

The field's greatest weakness is the significant uncertainty surrounding both the nature and timeline of risks, coupled with the early stage of proposed solutions. Experts disagree on when (or whether) transformative AI will arrive, what the main dangers will be, and which research paths are most promising. The technical work is highly speculative, with few clear metrics for progress, making it difficult to evaluate impact. Furthermore, the field faces challenges of talent constraints and academic credibility, with relatively few researchers having the necessary expertise. There are also concerns that research could unintentionally accelerate dangerous capabilities alongside safety work.

Given these uncertainties, donors have to be comfortable with a higher risk-reward profile than in more established cause areas, essentially betting on a particular vision of technological development that, while possible, remains speculative.

Farmed animal welfare

What is this cause area?

Farmed animal welfare focuses on reducing the suffering of animals raised for food. With over 80 billion land animals and trillions of aquatic animals farmed annually, the scale of potential suffering is immense. Most farmed animals are raised in industrial systems that are, at best, comparable to human prisons. Key interventions include corporate campaigns pressuring food companies to adopt higher welfare standards; legal advocacy for protective regulations; plant-based and cultivated meat development; and institutional outreach promoting welfare-focused policies.

The case for prioritizing this area rests on three things: the sheer number of animals affected, the severity of their suffering, and the neglect of animal-focused causes in philanthropy. Animal charities receive less than 1.5% of all donations, and farmed animals only receive a fraction of that, despite representing over 99% of animals used by humans. For donors focused on reducing suffering, farmed animal welfare offers an outstanding opportunity.

Example of a possible benchmark charity

The Humane League (THL) is one of the top-rated animal welfare charities, as rated by the animal welfare charity evaluator, Animal Charity Evaluators (ACE). THL runs strategic corporate campaigns, pressuring food companies to adopt higher welfare standards, particularly through cage-free and broiler chicken welfare commitments.

Their campaigns have shown impressive cost-effectiveness. ACE estimates that THL's work affects between eight and 120 animals per dollar donated. This means a $1 million donation could improve the welfare standards of eight to 120 million animals, making it extraordinarily cost-effective compared to many other interventions.

Other funders in this area

The funding landscape for farmed animal welfare is relatively small and concentrated. Coefficient Giving is the largest funder, contributing tens of millions annually to the space. The Effective Altruism Animal Welfare Fund pools smaller donations to support promising but often overlooked interventions. A number of family foundations have also stepped in, including the Greenbaum Foundation and the Navigation Fund. Despite recent growth, total philanthropic funding remains under $200 million a year (tiny, compared to other cause areas).

The biggest weakness of the area

The biggest weakness is how hard it is to measure impact. Rigorous studies are rare, mostly because the space is so underfunded. There's also the deeper philosophical question of whether animal suffering matters morally, which not all donors accept. The field faces fierce opposition from powerful agricultural interests with far more resources, and cultural attachment to meat consumption makes change hard. Welfare improvements also tend to raise production costs, which creates economic disincentives for companies to implement them, and makes traceability of progress more difficult.

Wildlife welfare

What is this cause area?

Wildlife welfare encompasses efforts to improve the well-being of animals living in natural environments, combining both traditional conservation approaches with emerging concerns about wild animal welfare more broadly. This includes protecting species and habitats both from human-caused threats and naturally occurring pain and suffering in the wild (e.g., parasites and disease). There are an enormous number of wild animals, so donors interested in this area could benefit billions to trillions of sentient beings. It considers how interventions impact individual animal well-being as well as the broader ecosystem.

Example of a great benchmark charity

Wild Animal Initiative exemplifies innovative work in this space by focusing on developing the scientific foundation for understanding and improving wild animal welfare. The organization conducts and funds pioneering research on welfare assessment, humane interventions, and welfare biology, exploring how ecological and evolutionary processes affect animal well-being. For approximately $1 million invested, Wild Animal Initiative can fund multiple research projects investigating welfare indicators across species, develop academic partnerships advancing welfare biology as a field, and create policy frameworks for welfare-conscious wildlife management.

Other funders in this area

The wildlife welfare funding landscape is very mixed. Certain animals get a disproportionate amount of attention: pandas, the iconic symbol of the World Wildlife Fund, get thousands of times more funding and attention than more endangered species like owl parrots. And both get more attention than the pain caused to common wild animals like pigeons or squirrels.

Traditional conservation funding comes from major environmental foundations like the Gordon and Betty Moore Foundation, MacArthur Foundation, and Wyss Foundation; government agencies like the U.S. Fish and Wildlife Service;

and large NGOs like the World Wildlife Fund and Nature Conservancy. The emerging wild animal welfare focus receives support primarily from effective-altruism-aligned funders, including the Animal Welfare Fund. Total philanthropic funding for wildlife preservation exceeds several billion dollars annually, but explicit wild animal welfare work receives only a few million dollars, reflecting its nascent status.

The biggest weakness of the area

The biggest weakness of wildlife welfare as a cause area is the deep uncertainty around which interventions work, driven by ecological complexity and limited research. Most natural systems involve intricate relationships where well-intentioned interventions could have cascading, unpredictable effects, potentially causing more harm than good. The field also faces measurement challenges in assessing wild animal welfare at scale, with limited tools for quantifying suffering across diverse species.

Climate change

What is this cause area?

Climate change philanthropy aims to mitigate global warming by reducing greenhouse gas emissions and building resilience to unavoidable climate effects. This area encompasses clean energy development, transportation electrification, agricultural reform, forest preservation, policy advocacy, and climate justice initiatives. The underlying theory holds that human-induced climate change presents an existential threat requiring rapid transitions away from fossil fuels and other high-emission activities. Climate philanthropy typically focuses on high-leverage opportunities that can catalyze broader changes through policy shifts, technological innovation, or market transformation.

Example of a great benchmark charity

The Good Food Institute (GFI) exemplifies effective climate work through its focus on transforming the global food system by promoting plant-based and cultivated meat alternatives. According to Giving Green assessments, a top evaluator in the climate charity space, food system interventions offer significant mitigation potential, as animal agriculture contributes approximately 15% of global emissions. For approximately $1 million invested, GFI can fund critical research advancing alternative proteins, support policy initiatives removing regulatory barriers, and engage with major food companies to accelerate market adoption. Alternative protein development represents a high-leverage opportunity, as the technological and economic barriers are lower than in sectors like heavy industry or transportation. Another clear standout charity is the Clean Air Task Force.

Other funders in this area

The climate funding landscape includes the ClimateWorks Foundation, which coordinates global grantmaking; the Bezos Earth Fund, which has pledged $10 billion over a decade; and Bloomberg Philanthropies' climate initiatives. Specialized funders like Breakthrough Energy focus on clean technology innovation, while others like the Climate Justice Resilience Fund prioritize vulnerable communities. Corporate climate commitments have increased dramatically, though the quality of implementation still varies widely. Despite growth, climate philanthropy receives only about 2% of total charitable giving in the U.S., and as Giving Green notes, funding remains concentrated in developed countries rather than emerging economies where emissions are growing fastest.

The biggest weakness of the area

The greatest weakness in climate philanthropy is the difficulty in attributing specific emissions reductions to particular interventions, given the complex, systemic nature of the challenge. Even organizations with strong theories of change face significant uncertainty about their actual impact. The vast scale of global emissions means that even successful interventions may appear minimal in percentage terms. Additionally, the field struggles with time-horizon challenges; the most important outcomes may take decades to manifest. Climate work also faces substantial political opposition from vested interests, creating implementation barriers even for technically sound solutions.

Pandemic preparedness and prevention

What is this cause area?

Pandemic preparedness and prevention focus on reducing the risks of catastrophic disease outbreaks through surveillance, research, capacity building, and policy development. This cause area encompasses efforts to detect emerging pathogens, develop medical countermeasures, strengthen health systems, and address biosecurity concerns. The underlying theory holds that while natural pandemics pose significant threats, advances in biotechnology may increase risks from engineered pathogens. The COVID-19 pandemic demonstrated both the enormous potential harm (millions of deaths, trillions in economic damage) and the inadequacy of existing prevention systems.

Example of a great benchmark charity

The Johns Hopkins Center for Health Security (CHS) exemplifies effective work in this space, using a multidisciplinary approach that combines research, policy development, and stakeholder education. CHS conducts rigorous analysis of biological threats, develops frameworks for pandemic preparedness, and convenes key decision-makers from government, industry, and civil society. For approximately $1 million invested, CHS can produce influential policy reports, run tabletop exercises simulating outbreak scenarios, and develop resources that shape national and international response strategies. Their work has directly informed U.S. pandemic planning and global health security frameworks. During COVID-19, CHS became a trusted source for tracking data and providing evidence-based recommendations.

Other funders in this area

The pandemic funding landscape includes the Gates Foundation funding vaccine development and global health security; Coefficient Giving investing in biosecurity; and the Rockefeller Foundation's pandemic prevention initiative. Government funding dominates the space, with agencies like BARDA and NIAID providing billions for research. New entities such as the Pandemic Fund at the World Bank and the Coalition for Epidemic Preparedness Innovations (CEPI) coordinate pooled resources. Despite increased attention post-COVID, funding remains cyclical, typically surging after outbreaks but diminishing as public attention wanes.

The biggest weakness of the area

The greatest weakness is the challenge of measuring the effectiveness of interventions aimed at preventing low-probability, infrequent events. Success often means "nothing happens," making impact evaluation inherently challenging and creating vulnerabilities to funding cuts when threats seem distant. The field is fragmented across global health, biosecurity, and animal-health domains, leading to potential gaps in effort. Pandemic work also faces political challenges, including nationalism that hinders international cooperation and bureaucratic inertia that slows the implementation of lessons learned.

High-income healthcare

What is this cause area?

High-income healthcare focuses on improving health outcomes in wealthy nations through both clinical interventions and broader well-being approaches. This cause area encompasses traditional medical care, mental health services, and preventive measures. Unlike global health, which often addresses basic needs through highly cost-effective interventions, high-income healthcare tends to involve more complex and expensive systems, serving populations with longer lifespans and different disease burdens, most commonly non-communicable diseases, mental health conditions, and age-related disorders.

Philanthropic efforts in this space often focus on addressing these disparities, promoting innovative delivery models, advancing specific research areas, or supporting prevention and wellness initiatives that fall outside traditional medical systems.

Example of a possible benchmark charity

Action for Happiness exemplifies an innovative approach in this space by focusing on mental well-being as both a health outcome and a determinant of physical health. The organization promotes evidence-based approaches to psychological wellness through education, community-building, and practical tools for improving mental health.

For approximately $1 million invested, Action for Happiness can run happiness skills courses reaching thousands of participants, support hundreds of community groups implementing well-being practices, and develop digital resources accessed by millions. Their impact evaluations show participants of courses reporting 20–35% improvements in mental well-being scores, with effects persisting months after program completion.

Other funders in this area

The high-income healthcare funding landscape is substantial but structured differently than other cause areas. Major philanthropic players include the Robert Wood Johnson Foundation, which focuses on healthcare systems and social determinants of health; the Commonwealth Fund, which supports research on healthcare access and quality; and condition-specific funders like the American Heart Association. Corporate foundations, particularly from pharmaceutical and insurance companies, direct significant resources toward specific disease areas. Mental health specifically receives disproportionately less funding relative to its disease burden, though this gap has narrowed in recent years.

The biggest weakness of the area

The greatest weakness of high-income healthcare as a cause area is its limited cost-effectiveness compared to interventions in lower-income settings or other cause areas. The marginal impact of additional resources is typically modest due to the law of diminishing returns in systems that already receive substantial funding. For example, extending life through high-income healthcare interventions often costs tens or hundreds of thousands of dollars per quality-adjusted life-year gained, compared to $50-200 in global health contexts. But it is a pretty strong choice if a donor wants to maximize their impact within their country.

High-income livelihoods

What is this cause area?

High-income livelihoods philanthropy focuses on improving economic opportunities and outcomes for people in wealthy nations through education, job training, career development, and related interventions. This area encompasses traditional educational initiatives, workforce development programs, entrepreneurship support, financial capability building, and efforts to address structural barriers to economic mobility. Unlike livelihoods work in developing countries, high-income interventions operate within complex, formalized economies with higher baseline education levels and different skills gaps. The field addresses challenges including technological disruption, growing inequality, declining economic mobility, and persistent disparities by race, geography, and socioeconomic status.

Example of a great benchmark charity

Year Up exemplifies effective work in this space through its intensive workforce development model serving young adults from underrepresented communities. The organization provides six months of technical and professional skills training followed by six-month corporate internships, creating pathways to living-wage careers. For approximately $1 million invested, Year Up can support roughly 40–50 participants through its full program, generating average annual earnings gains of $7,000–$8,000 per participant in the years following completion, a substantial 30–40% increase over control groups. These outcomes have been validated through randomized controlled trials, demonstrating sustained impact.

Other funders in this area

The high-income livelihoods funding landscape is diverse and substantial. Major philanthropic players include the Lumina Foundation and Gates Foundation, focusing on postsecondary education; the Markle Foundation and Strada Network investing in skills-based workforce development; and place-based funders like the Robin Hood Foundation addressing economic mobility in specific communities. Public funding dominates the space, with billions allocated to education, workforce development, and economic inclusion initiatives at the federal, state, and local levels.

The biggest weakness of the area

The greatest weakness of high-income livelihoods as a cause area is the difficulty in demonstrating cost-effectiveness relative to other philanthropic investments. Most interventions show modest impacts at relatively high costs, with successful programs like Year Up typically requiring thousands per participant. The field also faces substantial attribution challenges, as outcomes are influenced by broader economic conditions, individual characteristics, and numerous other factors beyond specific interventions. The evidence base remains mixed, with many common approaches (like brief job training programs) showing disappointing results in rigorous evaluations.

Human services and social justice

What is this cause area?

Human services and social justice philanthropy address systemic inequalities and provide direct support to marginalized populations. This broad cause area encompasses interventions ranging from immediate needs provision (food, shelter, healthcare access) to structural change efforts (criminal justice reform, voting rights, economic mobility). The underlying theory holds that societal systems perpetuate inequalities based on race, gender, class, disability, and other characteristics, requiring both direct services to address immediate suffering and advocacy to transform root causes. Unlike some cause areas with narrower focuses, human services/social justice work spans multiple domains, including education, healthcare, housing, employment, and civic participation. The field increasingly emphasizes shifting power to affected communities through participatory grantmaking, general operating support, and movement building rather than imposing external solutions.

Example of a possible benchmark charity

The Equal Justice Initiative (EJI) exemplifies effective work in this space, combining direct service with systemic change efforts. Founded by Bryan Stevenson, EJI provides legal representation to people wrongly convicted, unfairly sentenced, or abused in jails and prisons, while simultaneously working to transform the criminal justice system. For approximately $1 million invested, EJI can provide legal representation to dozens of individuals facing excessive punishments, potentially saving hundreds of years of inappropriate incarceration. These funds also support research that documents systemic abuses, public education campaigns reaching millions, and advocacy efforts that have helped change laws and policies affecting thousands.

Other funders in this area

The human services/social justice funding landscape is diverse but unevenly distributed. Major institutional supporters include Ford Foundation, which has committed its entire grantmaking to addressing inequality; Open Society Foundations, which focuses on democratic governance and justice; and the MacArthur Foundation's criminal justice reform initiative. Community foundations direct significant resources to local human services organizations, while United Way represents a major funding intermediary. Public funding through government contracts remains essential for many direct service providers.

The biggest weakness of the area

The primary weakness in this cause area is the difficulty in measuring the long-term impact of interventions addressing complex, multifaceted problems with numerous contributing factors. Most of these interventions have a limited evidence base, and they tend to be more expensive than those focused on health or economic outcomes. There are also major disagreements about which populations are most in need, with most social justice organizations still taking a primarily local perspective, focusing on vulnerable groups within high-income countries.

The arts

What is this cause area?

The arts as a cause area encompasses supporting and expanding access to visual arts, music, literature, dance, theater, film, and other creative expressions. Arts philanthropy typically aims to preserve cultural heritage, foster creativity, provide educational opportunities, and increase accessibility for underserved communities. The case for supporting the arts includes their intrinsic value through aesthetic experience; their instrumental benefits, such as improved educational outcomes, community cohesion, and economic development; and their transformative potential to challenge perspectives and inspire social change.

Example of a possible benchmark charity

Americans for the Arts and the National Endowment for the Arts (NEA) are leading organizations in this space. Americans for the Arts conducts research, advocacy, and professional development to strengthen the arts ecosystem nationwide. The NEA functions as a critical grantmaker with rigorous evaluation processes. For approximately $1 million invested, organizations like these can support dozens of community arts programs serving hundreds of participants, fund research demonstrating arts' societal benefits, or provide operational support to cultural institutions in underserved areas. While impact metrics differ from those used in health or economic interventions, studies show that arts programs can sometimes produce meaningful outcomes, such as 10–15% improvements in academic performance among youth and up to a 30% reduction in recidivism through prison arts programs.

Other funders in this area

The arts funding landscape includes many private foundations like Ford, Andrew W. Mellon, and Bloomberg Philanthropies; corporate foundations such as Bank of America and Target; and public agencies, including state and local arts councils. Community foundations often dedicate significant portions of their grantmaking to local arts initiatives. Crowdfunding platforms have emerged as increasingly important for independent artists and smaller organizations. Despite this diversity, arts funding faces geographic disparities, with rural and economically disadvantaged communities receiving disproportionately less support than wealthy urban centers.

The biggest weakness of the area

The greatest weakness of arts philanthropy is the difficulty of demonstrating objective impact, especially compared to interventions with clear metrics like lives saved or income increased. There are also substantial debates about how much good the arts create, particularly when funding goes to high-income-focused institutions like opera houses or art museums, while more essential needs like food or healthcare remain unmet in other communities. Few people, when faced with the choice between a hospital bill and an arts expense, would prioritize the latter.

Appendix H: Open vs. Closed Applications

A key strategic decision for your foundation is whether your grant-sourcing process should be open or closed. In other words, do you source opportunities using an application process that is open to the public or through your network?

Open application processes could involve a general application form or a request for proposals that is open and advertised to the public. Closed application processes could involve inviting members of the foundation's network to make a general application or respond to a private request for proposals, or receiving referrals for good projects or people through members of the network. There are advantages and disadvantages to each grant-sourcing approach; ultimately, it is likely that your grantmaking will incorporate elements of both. However, we believe there is a lot of value in some degree of open sourcing, provided the foundation has the capacity to vet a potentially high volume of applications. Let's take a deeper look at why.

Relative advantages

Many foundations default to the type of application process they find most convenient, without considering all of their relative advantages and disadvantages.

	Open process	Closed process
Main capacity required from the foundation	Effective outreach strategy for the sourcing of candidates **Time-efficient vetting system**	**Strong, differentiated network** or outreach capability to source candidates that are competitive with the best in an open process Effective enough vetting system and **discipline not to grant if below a certain benchmark**
Resource intensity	**High** (Foundations: assessing applications; Applicants: writing applications)	**Lower/flexible** (as much networking and outreach as the foundation would like)
Opportunity pool	**Large** and **diverse**	**Small** and **more uniform**
Risk of bias	**Lower**	**Higher**
Systematic	**More**	**Less** effort to make more systematic

Most foundations today source opportunities via a closed approach. Meanwhile, in our experience, roughly 20% of charities tend to make up roughly 80% of the attendees at major conferences and networking events. As a result, the average foundation using a closed applications approach is likely to end up granting to this particularly well-networked 20%. For these foundations, the impact of their granting is lower: if they hadn't donated to one of these particularly well-networked charities, someone else probably would have. Consequently, in closed grant-sourcing, the impact is only high for foundations with a differentiated network that can find opportunities that wouldn't have been funded otherwise.

Foundations considering an open grant-sourcing approach, on the other hand, should consider whether this has a strong impact given their scope. If your foundation runs an open process that seeks grant applications within the same scope (cause area, location, org size, etc.), the best applications in your process may have otherwise been funded by the other foundations' processes. In open grant sourcing, counterfactual impact is highest when the foundation's scope doesn't completely overlap with another organization, especially if it also has a well-run open application process.

Real-world examples

Open: EA Funds

EA Funds invites applications from anyone who thinks their project could be highly impactful and cost-effective within the scope of one of four funds.

Fund	Focuses on:	Usually supports:	Decided using:
Global health and development fund	Funding outstanding, evidence-based opportunities to provide better access to healthcare and economic development where it's needed most	Established organizations	Scientific evidence and fund managers' judgment

Animal welfare fund	Funding organizations and projects that will help alleviate the suffering of millions or billions of animals	Early-stage and established organizations	Organizational track record and fund managers' judgment
Long-term future fund	Funding to people or projects that aim to improve the long-term future, such as by reducing risks from artificial intelligence and engineered pandemics	Individuals and organizations (includes speculative opportunities)	Fund managers' judgment
Effective Altruism infrastructure fund	Funding to organizations or people that aim to grow or improve the effective altruism community	Organizations and early-stage projects (includes speculative opportunities)	Fund managers' judgment

Despite having an open application process, EA puts few resources into advertising it. This may be because, without much active promotion, it receives several hundred applications per year. To minimize the resource intensity associated with processing applications, EA:

a) Tries to be crystal clear about the scope of projects it funds; applicants even have to tick a box confirming that they have read and understood the scope. This saves the time of applicants who aren't a good fit, and saves fund managers' time processing applications. At the same time, EA avoids being overly narrow or prescriptive in its stated scope, because "having too-prescriptive rules could lead to grant applicants (intentionally or unintentionally) modifying their applications to game the system by conforming to what they expect fund managers will be more likely to recommend grants to, rather than applying for the thing that they actually care about."[72]

b) Sets a limit of 5,000 characters for the initial application, recommending that applicants use many fewer and spend just one or two hours on the application.

c) Has applicants fill out a prescriptive application form, rather than create their own. This makes the systematic comparison of applicants faster.

d) Has created a help center on their website with answers to frequently asked questions to reduce the administrative burden.

Closed: Mulago Foundation

The Mulago Foundation has no channel for members of the public to apply for funding. The reason is that proposals take a lot of work without providing the needed information. Instead, it sources proposals through its network.[73] It has taken the Foundation time to build a portfolio of recipient organizations through this grant-sourcing process, which is inherently less scalable than EA Funds' open application process. However, Mulago has amassed over 70 recipient organizations that it has enough confidence in to invest in long-term. It also runs several fellowship programs, which aim to find leaders with promising solutions that Mulago can help to design and scale. Similarly to their grantmaking, there is no open application process; potential participants for the fellowships are headhunted by Mulago staff or referred by its network.

A bit of both: Unorthodox Philanthropy

As the name suggests, Unorthodox Philanthropy (UP) does things differently from most foundations. Its grantmaking process is structured as a series of experiments that it uses to determine the best way to operate, and it runs funding rounds (called "searches") focused on topics like "endgames with finite capital" and "extraordinary leaders transforming a field" rather than focusing on specific cause areas or types of interventions.

UP's creativity has allowed it to identify and support some great opportunities before other foundations. For example, the winner of its first search was GiveDirectly, which gives unconditional cash transfers, a relatively controversial idea in 2010. GiveDirectly is now seen by many as *the* intervention to beat in the global health and development space.

Because its approach is experimental by nature, UP's position on the open/closed grantmaking spectrum has changed over time:

- Its first search was structured as a winner-takes-all competition, with applicants competing for a single grant prize.

- The second search was structured as a more typical open application process; the foundation received 1,000 submissions, of which it shortlisted 150 and awarded grants to 18. However, it was noticed that the majority of applications came from its existing networks, suggesting that the open-application approach was not necessarily generating a broader pool of opportunities than a closed system. Subsequently, it resolved to invest more energy in reaching out to communities without the ears of private philanthropists.

- Its third search, focused on the COVID response, was closed, sourcing grants from its network to respond rapidly to a time-sensitive problem.

- UP's latest search is experimenting with a nomination process instead of individuals applying on their own behalf.

Experimenting in your grantmaking takes effort and makes it more difficult to build up expertise in any one approach. But it has the potential to be extremely beneficial. Most importantly, perhaps, it could help you to figure out the best approach for *you*, rather than just picking one system and hoping for the best.

Appendix I: Counterfactuals in Funding Decisions

The final step in defining a strong strategy for your foundation is to consider your counterfactual impact. We've mentioned counterfactual impact in passing several times so far in this handbook, but now we will explore it in more detail.

Counterfactual thinking considers the hypothetical question of how things would have played out differently if something that happened in reality had not happened.

When thinking about making a positive impact on the world in a consequentialist fashion, most people take the consequences that follow from their actions at face value. For example, imagine that Tom was trying to decide whether to have a positive impact by becoming a surgeon or by working in finance and donating to effective global health charities. A heart surgeon's impact appears to be saving the lives of each patient, while a donor to the Against Malaria Foundation appears to have the impact of saving one life from malaria per ~$5,000 donated.

Thinking counterfactually about impact, Tom would ask: If he doesn't study medicine, will the patients die? Probably not. Medicine is highly competitive, and if Tom doesn't do it, it is highly probable that another person just as capable would take his place. On the other hand, if Tom had not donated to the Against Malaria Foundation (AMF), would the beneficiaries have been prevented from dying of malaria? Considering that AMF still has a sizable funding gap, the answer to this question is probably not. To be more certain that he will actually save a life, Tom should donate to AMF. Thinking about impact in terms of what would have happened otherwise generally leads one to apply a discount to their estimate of how much impact their actions will actually generate. However, it is a far more consequential and realistic picture of the impact of your actions.

In the context of grantmaking, there are many counterfactual questions to consider, but two stick out:

(1) If I don't fund this grant, will someone else fund it anyway?

(2) If this grant application doesn't get funded, how will the recipient's impact be different?

Let's look at these questions in more detail, using an example.

Imagine a young global health charity with two proposed programs designed to combat parasitic worm infections in children. One program distributes deworming medication in schools and is highly impactful; the other aims to educate families on how to avoid infection and is ineffective. Suppose the charity is applying for a grant to fund the highly impactful program.

If I don't fund this grant, will someone else fund it anyway?

- In some cases, the grant applicant plans to apply to a number of foundations and government schemes, and their application will be attractive to many of these potential funders. In this case, if you choose not to fund the grant, the grant will probably be funded anyway, significantly discounting the impact of your funding decision.

- In other cases, the grant application will not be attractive or in scope for most funders in the landscape, or the applicant lacks the confidence/network/resources to pursue funding from other sources. In this case, if you choose not to fund the grant, it probably won't get funded at all, meaning deciding to fund it has a significant counterfactual impact.

If this grant application doesn't get funded, how will the recipient's impact be different?

- In some cases, if a grant application doesn't get funded, the applicant will move their budget around between programs so that they can still execute the program. If our example charity did this, the impactful program would still be funded, and the ineffective one would not be. In this case, there is little to no counterfactual impact from the grant being funded.

- On the other hand, in many cases, a specific grant not being funded means a specific program not being executed, or being executed on a smaller scale. In this case, there is a significant counterfactual impact from the grant being funded.

- Moreover, for small/early organizations, not receiving funding for a particular grant could be the difference between that organization continuing to operate or having to shut down. In this case, the counterfactual impact of funding the grant is not just the additional medication distribution that the grant pays for but also the lifetime impact the organization might achieve by continuing to operate.

As a grantmaker, you need to consider the likelihood of these kinds of scenarios when deciding whether to fund a grant. It helps to have a strong understanding of the landscape and your competitive advantage as a funder: Who are the other funders who are likely to fund similar projects to you? What types of projects are particularly attractive or unattractive to them? How do your capabilities (e.g., network, subject-matter expertise) overlap, and how do they differ? How do your values, worldviews, and approaches to vetting differ, and where might they result in gaps? What types of projects tend to be neglected by funders? As a result, what types of projects are you uniquely qualified to discover and vet?

Figuring out counterfactual impact precisely is difficult. A decision to do or not to do something has cascading effects; think of how dropping a pebble in a lake sends rings propagating out across the lake's surface. So far, we have just discussed the first of these rings. Let's go further out:

Consider a promising grant application that you choose to fund, but which would have been funded by another foundation if you hadn't funded it. The first level of counterfactual thinking would suggest that you achieved no real impact by funding the grant. But because you funded the grant, you displaced another foundation that will now probably spend that money elsewhere. If that other foundation is effective at grantmaking, it will probably fund another strong opportunity, which may displace another foundation's funding. This process can continue, with the consequences of your decision to fund a promising grant rippling out across the funding "lake." When thinking counterfactually, remember not to discount the impact of funding projects that would have been funded otherwise, and avoid applying zero discounting to the impact of funding projects that wouldn't have been funded otherwise.

When it comes to applying counterfactual thinking in the real world, some strange scenarios arise that can easily lead to incorrect appraisals of your impact. For example, if only 90% of the funding needed to start a project has been raised, does donating the last 10% mean you should get full credit for the project, or 10% of the credit? Counting the full impact seems sensible using counterfactual thinking, but it will lead to double-counting between different organizations (the foundation that donated 90% is unlikely to take 0% credit for the organization's founding). Dividing impact proportionally can make sense in some cases, but it can result in leverage not being accurately taken into account. One possible solution is to use a formal methodology, like a Shapley value, a solution concept used in game theory that involves fairly distributing both gains and costs to several actors working in coalition. A simpler heuristic might be to hold your counterfactual views lightly and to fund the best projects you can, even if there is some concern that they would be supported by other funders.

In the end, when the goal is positive impact, all that matters is that charity funders collectively find and fund the best opportunities. A way to help make this happen is by increasing donor coordination so that funders make better decisions collectively.

Donor coordination and funding circles

What does an ideal funding landscape look like?

The funding landscapes in most cause areas leave plenty of room for improve-ment. Funders often lack a deep awareness of each other, resulting in limited information sharing, and great organizations frequently fall through the cracks. A more effective structure would provide a clear pathway for organizations to scale up, transitioning from smaller to larger funders. A diverse range of informed funders would share notes and information with each other. This would enable them to notice the gaps between them and avoid missed opportunities. Shared information and perspective would hopefully mean their scopes would overlap somewhat, with high-impact organizations in their cause area always getting the necessary funding. One structure that does these things well is funding circles (see Appendix F).

Summary

- Counterfactuals refer to hypothetical scenarios of what might have occurred if certain conditions had been different. Two main questions about counterfactuals that are significant for a foundation's impact:

    (1) If I don't fund this grant, will someone else fund it anyway? *If so, the impact of funding the grant is significantly lower.*

    (2) If this grant application doesn't get funded, how will the recipient's impact be different? *If they are able to reallocate existing funds to carry out the intervention, the impact of funding the grant is relatively low. If they are dependent on the grant to carry out the intervention, the impact is relatively high. If receiving the grant could determine whether the organization can continue to operate or is forced to shut down, the impact could be especially high.*

- When thinking through these counterfactual scenarios, it helps to have a strong understanding of the landscape and your competitive advantage as a funder. Ask yourself questions, including: Which other funders are likely to fund similar projects to yours? What types of projects are particularly attractive or unattractive to them? How do your capabilities overlap and differ? What types of projects are you uniquely qualified to discover and vet?

Appendix J: Small Foundation, Big Impact

Why start a foundation with a relatively small amount of money?

A discouraging sentiment can often be found in philanthropy: "Very large foundations have all the impact." After all, what can a $1 million-a-year donation do if there is a player in the space that gives 100 times that? Although it's important to face harsh realities, we do not believe this is one of them. Foundations of different sizes have different natural strengths and weaknesses. Let's look at why small foundations can have an outsized impact.

1. Small funders play an important role in nurturing smaller, early-stage organizations.

A massive foundation like GiveWell, with its highly rigorous vetting system, invests so many resources into each grant decision that it can only consider mature organizations that can absorb tens of millions in additional funding. But assessing smaller, less mature organizations is also very important, because: (a)

If no one supports early-stage organizations, they will never become mature enough for large foundations, and (b) there are many impactful opportunities that aren't scalable enough to be supported by the largest foundations.

In this way, small and large foundations are complementary parts of the nonprofit ecosystem.

2. Foundations can have an impact beyond their funding.

Any foundation has the opportunity to become a thought leader in the philanthropic community. It can put forward new grantmaking strategies that haven't been considered, promote better norms (like requiring grant recipients to invest energy in monitoring and evaluation), or bring attention to a neglected problem or intervention. This opportunity is available to small and large foundations alike, and foundations are often able to punch well above their weight. For example, the Mulago Foundation has been a prominent voice in the discourse on how to increase the impact of the nonprofit sector, including writing a methodology and publishing free tools to assist charities in defining an explicit strategy to scale.

3. Being small comes with other comparative advantages, such as:

a. **Generalized staff:** Large foundations tend to specialize their grantmaking staff. There are advantages to this, but the generalists at smaller foundations are better able to apply lessons from one field to another, and to fund things that fall through the cracks between specialties.

b. **Ability to take risks:** Big grantmakers have big reputations and have to be careful that grantmaking in one field does not affect their grantmaking in others. This leads them to be more risk-averse than smaller foundations (and some high-risk projects have very high potential for impact).

c. **Ability to capture time-sensitive opportunities:** Small foundations are nimbler and less bureaucratic than larger ones, so they're better able to respond quickly to time-sensitive opportunities, such as natural disasters, a pandemic outbreak, or a sudden policy window. They are also able to pivot much more quickly if evidence comes to light that shows the direction they are headed is not as impactful as previously thought.

Here's an example of when a smaller foundation has an advantage over a large one: Imagine two foundations that both finance microcredit interventions. Foundation A has four staff members, deploying $2 million in funding each year.

Foundation B employs 30 staff members and deploys $50 million per year. Now let's say a large meta-analysis is done on microcredit.[74] The results of the data are disappointing, showing far fewer effects than either foundation had hoped for.

Foundation A's response to this situation is relatively simple. It gathers its four staff members together to talk about the findings. Although some of the staffers have to revise their assumptions more than others, they are all working in multiple areas, and deprioritizing microcredit gives them more capacity to expand their work elsewhere. They do not have a large number of long-term commitments in the space, and the organizations they fund would survive without them. Relatively quickly, they come up with a transition plan to move away from the area over the next six months.

Over in the office of Foundation B, it's a different matter. Fifteen of the staff do not do any work in microcredit and thus did not even see the analysis. Of the five staffers who read it, three of them are working full-time on microcredit and have been in the field for years. Deprioritizing the area would likely result in them quitting or being fired. In addition, they have made large and public commitments to the area. Moving out of the space would have major ramifications, not just on those they grant to, but on the area as a whole. Several meetings later, the director of the foundation makes a call that they will fund their own two-year analysis of the area and re-evaluate at that point. Until then, they will maintain, but not grow, their grantmaking in the area. If the foundation then leaves the area, it will have a three-year transition period, allowing the field to stabilize without its presence.

These are very different outcomes, even though these two foundations share the same values and responded rationally to the same evidence. One foundation leaves the area fully in six months, and the other stays for at least five more years. This scenario, similar to the advantage a new for-profit startup has over a large, established company, highlights the value of small foundations.

Appendix K: Glossary

Charities: Organizations similar to NGOs (see below), with some countries having stricter legal requirements around charities due to higher levels of tax deductibility. Throughout this book, the terms charity and NGO are used interchangeably.

DALY (Disability-Adjusted Life Year): A standardized metric used in health economics to quantify disease burden. One DALY represents the loss of one year of healthy life, combining years lost due to premature mortality and years lived with disability. Widely used by the World Health Organization and in cost-effectiveness analyses to compare health interventions.

Foundations: Private philanthropic organizations that distribute grants and funding to support charitable causes, research, and social initiatives. They typically operate with endowments or ongoing funding from individuals, families, or corporations, playing a crucial role in providing financial resources to NGOs and other charitable organizations.

Grantmaker: Includes private foundations, governments, and high-net-worth donors who provide grants to charities and NGOs. This broad category encompasses all entities that formally distribute funding to nonprofit organizations. Grantmaker and foundation are both used fairly interchangeably in this book.

Hedonic Adaptation: A psychological phenomenon by which individuals return to a relatively stable baseline level of happiness despite positive or negative life events. Also known as the "hedonic treadmill," this concept has important implications for program design and impact measurement, suggesting that subjective well-being gains from interventions may fade over time as people adapt to new circumstances.

NGOs (Non-Governmental Organizations): Private, typically nonprofit organizations that operate independently from government control to address social, environmental, humanitarian, or development issues. They range from small community-based organizations to large international entities, often serving as intermediaries between donors and beneficiaries.

M&E (Monitoring and Evaluation): A systematic approach to tracking and assessing program performance, effectiveness, and impact. Monitoring involves ongoing data collection to track progress, while evaluation involves periodic assessment of whether interventions achieve intended outcomes. Essential for evidence-based decision making and organizational learning.

Veil of Ignorance: A philosophical thought experiment by John Rawls, where individuals design principles for a just society without knowing their own position within it. In development and grantmaking contexts, this framework suggests prioritizing interventions that help the most disadvantaged globally, since rational decision-makers would choose policies that are fair regardless of their eventual social position.

Randomized Controlled Trials (RCTs): A research methodology considered the gold standard for establishing causal relationships between interventions and outcomes. Participants are randomly assigned to treatment or control groups, with all other factors held constant. This eliminates selection bias and allows researchers to isolate the true impact of interventions, helping organizations make evidence-based decisions about program effectiveness.

SMART Goals: A framework for setting effective objectives where goals are Specific, Measurable, Achievable, Relevant, and Time-bound. This methodology helps organizations create actionable targets that can be tracked and evaluated for progress and success.

Endnotes

1   Livelihood Impact Fund, "How We Fund," accessed November 4, 2025, www.livelihoodimpactfund.org/how-we-fund

2   Happier Lives Institute, "The Wellbeing Cost-Effectiveness of StrongMinds and Friendship Bench: Combining a Systematic Review and Meta-Analysis with Charity-Related Data (Nov 2024 Update)," accessed November 4, 2025, www.happierlivesinstitute.org/report/the-wellbeing-cost-effectiveness-of-strongminds-and-friendship-bench-combining-a-systematic-review-and-meta-analysis-with-charity-related-data-nov-2024-update/.

3   International Rescue Committee, "Cost Efficiency: Legal Case Management," accessed November 4, 2025, www.rescue.org/report/cost-efficiency-legal-case-management.

4   Mieux Donner, "How We Calculate the Impact of Carbon Reduction," accessed November 4, 2025, mieuxdonner.org/how-we-calculate-the-impact-of-carbon-reduction/.

5   Artis Foundation, "Do the Arts Perform at School?" PDF, May 2024, artisfoundation.org.uk/wp-content/uploads/2024/05/Do-the-arts-perform-at-school.pdf, accessed November 4, 2025.

6   GiveWell, "Against Malaria Foundation," December 2023, www.givewell.org/charities/amf, accessed November 4, 2025.

7   Helen Kissel, "Open Philanthropy Shallow Investigation: Tobacco Control," Effective Altruism Forum, January 25, 2023, forum.effectivealtruism.org/posts/bfJPcHqDXb5yp2zXo, accessed November 4, 2025.

8   Action for Happiness, "Course Evaluation," accessed November 4, 2025, legacy.actionforhappiness.org/course-evaluation.

9   Vicky Cox, "Structured Pedagogy to Increase Education Quality," Charity Entrepreneurship, August 2024, 370b8129-500b-4a5d99f2-ce6886702186.usrfiles.com/ugd/370b81_1885f40e02af4286a00811162be9b0b3.pdf, accessed November 4, 2025.

10   Harry J. Holzer, "Should the Federal Government Spend More on Workforce Development?," Brookings Institution, May 23, 2023, www.brookings.edu/articles/should-the-federal-government-spend-more-on-workforce-development/, accessed November 4, 2025.

11   Lant Pritchett, "The Perils of Partial Attribution: Let's All Play for Team Development," Center for Global Development, October 26, 2017, www.cgdev.org/publication/perils-partial-attribution, accessed November 27, 2025.

12   Open Philanthropy, "Biosecurity," January 11, 2014, www.openphilanthropy.org/research/biosecurity/, accessed November 4, 2025.

13   John Halstead, "Climate Change Cause Area Report," Founders Pledge, May 2018, www.founderspledge.com/downloads/fp-climate-change, accessed November 4, 2025.

14   Animal Charity Evaluators, "Çiftlik Hayvanlarını Koruma Derneği: Charity Review," May 2024, animalcharityevaluators.org/charity-review/ciftlik-hayvanlarini-koruma-dernegi/, accessed November 4, 2025.

15   Animal Charity Evaluators, "Wild Animal Initiative: Charity Review," 2023, animalcharityevaluators.org/charity-review/wild-animal-initiative/, accessed November 4, 2025.

16   John Roman, "Cost-Benefit Analysis of Criminal Justice Reforms," National Institute of Justice Journal, no. 272 (September 2013), www.ojp.gov/pdffiles1/nij/241929.pdf, accessed November 4, 2025.

17   Holden Karnofsky, "Potential Risks from Advanced Artificial Intelligence: The Philanthropic Opportunity," Open Philanthropy, May 6, 2016, www.openphilanthropy.org/research/potential-risks-from-advanced-artificial-intelligence-the-philanthropic-opportunity/, accessed November 4, 2025.

18   P.S. ARTS, "Membership," accessed November 4, 2025, psarts.org/membership/

19   Internal analysis (unpublished). www.issuelab.org/resources/44233/44233.pdf (accessed November 4, 2025).

20 Spencer Fraseur, The Irrational Mind: How to Fight Back Against the Hidden Forces That Affect Decision Making (SF Publishing, 2020).

21 Agency Fund, "Join Us," accessed July 5, 2025, www.agency.fund/join-us.

22 EA Funds, "Animal Welfare Fund," accessed July 5, 2025, funds.effectivealtruism.org/funds/animal-welfare.

23 Bloom Wellbeing Fund, accessed July 5, 2025, bloomwellbeing.fund.

24 "Grants scorecard WFM template 2024 (template)," Google Sheets spreadsheet, accessed November 4, 2025, docs.google.com/spreadsheets/d/1ONpl2tsKLoJKbDz7-Y513u4fb4hrN-aG-lkGnzt7czk/.

25 Open Philanthropy, accessed November 4, 2025, www.openphilanthropy.org/.

26 Impactful Grantmaking, accessed November 4, 2025, impactfulgrantmaking.com.

27 Alex Singal and Tracy Williams, "GiveWell as Moneyball," GiveWell Blog, September 17, 2024, blog.givewell.org/2024/09/17/givewell-as-moneyball/, accessed November 4, 2025.

28 Luke Muehlhauser, "Reasoning Transparency," Open Philanthropy, December 1, 2017, www.openphilanthropy.org/research/reasoning-transparency/, accessed November 4, 2025.

29 Ray Dalio, "Principles for Success," YouTube video, May 21, 2018, www.youtube.com/watch?v=B9XGUpQZY38, accessed November 4, 2025.

30 Dan Pink, "The Surprising Truth about What Animates Us," RSA Animate, April 1, 2010, www.youtube.com/watch?v=u6XAPnuFjJc, accessed November 4, 2025.

31 Animal Charity Evaluators, "Why Farmed Animals?," accessed November 4, 2025, animalcharityevaluators.org/charity-reviews/causes-we-consider/why-farmed-animals/.

32 Boris Yakubchik, "It Is Effectiveness, not Overhead that Matters," 80,000 Hours Blog, November 4, 2011, 80000hours.org/2011/11/it-is-effectiveness-not-overhead-that-matters/, accessed November 4, 2025.

33 Ozzie Gooen, "Visual Sensitivity Analysis in Guesstimate," The Guesstimate Blog (Medium), May 17, 2016, medium.com/guesstimate-blog/analysis-view-with-guesstimate-4afadd87f72c, accessed November 4, 2025.

34 "Scope neglect," Wikipedia, last modified January 29, 2023, en.wikipedia.org/wiki/Scope_neglect, accessed November 4, 2025.

35 Alexander Berger, "Errors in DCP2 cost-effectiveness estimate for deworming," GiveWell Blog, September 29, 2011, blog.givewell.org/2011/09/29/errors-in-dcp2-cost-effectiveness-estimate-for-deworming/, accessed November 4, 2025.

36 GiveWell, "Research on Moral Weights: 2019," accessed November 4, 2025, www.givewell.org/how-we-work/our-criteria/cost-effectiveness/2019-moral-weights-research.

37 Holden Karnofsky, "Why We Can't Take Expected Value Estimates Literally (Even When They're Unbiased)," GiveWell Blog, August 18, 2011, blog.givewell.org/2011/08/18/why-we-cant-take-expected-value-estimates-literally-even-when-theyre-unbiased/, accessed November 4, 2025.

38 Saulius Šimčikas, "List of Ways in Which Cost-Effectiveness Estimates Can Be Misleading," Effective Altruism Forum, August 20, 2019, forum.effectivealtruism.org/posts/zdAst6ezi45cChRi6, accessed November 4, 2025.

39 Hazelfire, "Type Checking GiveWell's GiveDirectly Cost-Effective Analysis," Effective Altruism Forum, June 23, 2021, forum.effectivealtruism.org/posts/WmQwtYEajNDuPdyZx, accessed November 4, 2025.

40 See, for example, Joel McGuire, Samuel Dupret, and Michael Plant, "Deworming and decay: replicating GiveWell's cost-effectiveness analysis," Effective Altruism Forum, July 25, 2022, forum.effectivealtruism.org/posts/MKiqGvijAXfcBHCYJ, accessed November 4, 2025.

41 Saulius Šimčikas, "List of Ways in Which Cost-Effectiveness Estimates Can Be Misleading," Effective Altruism Forum, August 20, 2019, forum. effectivealtruism.org/posts/zdAst6ezi45cChRi6, accessed November 4, 2025.

42 Joshua A. Salomon et al., "Common Values in Assessing Health Outcomes from Disease and Injury: Disability Weights Measurement Study for the Global Burden of Disease Study 2010," Lancet 380, no. 9859 (December 15, 2012): 2129-43, doi.org/10.1016/S0140-6736(12)61680-8.

43 Daniel Gilbert et al., "Immune Neglect: A Source of Durability Bias in Affective Forecasting," Journal of Personality and Social Psychology 75, no. 3 (January 1, 1998): 617-38, doi.org/10.1037/0022-3514.75.3.617.

44 GiveWell, "Approaches to Moral Weights: How GiveWell Compares to Other Actors," 2020, www.givewell.org/how-we-work/our-criteria/cost-effectiveness/comparing-moral-weights, accessed November 4, 2025.

45 Derek, "Health and Happiness Research Topics, Part 1: Background on QALYs and DALYs," Effective Altruism Forum, December 9, 2020, forum.effectivealtruism.org/posts/Lncdn3tXi2aRt56k5, accessed November 4, 2025.

46 Michael Plant, "The Measurement of Wellbeing," Happier Lives Institute, www.happierlivesinstitute.org/report/the-measurement-of-wellbeing/, accessed November 4, 2025.

47 Joel McGuire, Samuel Dupret, and Michael Plant, "To WELLBY or Not to WELLBY? Measuring Non-Health, Non-Pecuniary Benefits Using Subjective Wellbeing," Effective Altruism Forum, August 11, 2022, forum. effectivealtruism.org/posts/dk48Sn6hpbMWeJo4G, accessed November 4, 2025.

48 Charity Entrepreneurship, "Is It Better to Be a Wild Rat or a Factory Farmed Cow? A Systematic Method for Comparing Animal Welfare," September 16, 2018, www.charityentrepreneurship.com/post/is-it-better-to-be-a-wild-rat-or-a-factory-farmed-cow-a-systematic-method-for-comparing-animal-welfare, accessed November 4, 2025.

49 This welfare score reflects quality of life, but it does not incorporate the probability that different species are sentient in the first place, or how intensely they are capable of suffering or experiencing pleasure (which you might call their "welfare range"). Other organizations have explored these variables, for example Rethink Priorities' work on sentience probabilities, which can be combined with welfare points to allow for better cross-species comparisons.

50 David Pilling, The Growth Delusion: Wealth, Poverty, and the Well-Being of Nations (Crown, 2019).

51 Practitioners do this either through time discounting, through modeling only a fixed number of years (for example, 20), or through both approaches. We recommend using a consistent approach in all your CEAs (cost-effectiveness analyses) so that you compare like with like. In GiveWell's 2023 CEAs, they apply a time discount to benefits (4 percent annually) and model different benefits for a fixed number of years based on the research (for example, for AMF (Against Malaria Foundation) they model income benefits as lasting 40 years; for GiveDirectly they model income benefits from investing cash transfers as accruing for 10 years).

52 A normal distribution assumes the highest concentration of values around one average, with tails tapering off at either end.

53 A Z-score is, roughly, a measure of how far a data point is from the mean.

54 These charities provide children with tablets that treat parasitic worm infections that cause diseases such as schistosomiasis and helminthiasis.

55 Holden Karnofsky, "Sequence Thinking vs. Cluster Thinking (Oversimplified)," GiveWell Blog, June 10, 2014, blog.givewell. org/2014/06/10/sequence-thinking-vs-cluster-thinking/, accessed November 4, 2025.

56 Scale can influence modeled cost-effectiveness because a higher prevalence of an issue (for example, the percentage of people contracting malaria) can make the same intervention (for example, a bed net) produce a larger benefit for the same cost. A larger overall problem size can also allow a charity to spread fixed costs (such as headquarters office

costs and accounting) across more delivered impact, increasing cost-effectiveness. Scale can matter for a grantmaker's own effort as well. A grantmaker can deploy $10 million more quickly, and with lower decision costs, by funding one large project rather than one hundred smaller projects with similar cost-effectiveness. This is particularly relevant for grantmakers aiming to deploy very large amounts each year.

57 This is due to the statistical phenomenon of regression to the mean.

58 Alana Petraske, "Comparing Foundation Minimum Distribution in the US, Canada, and the UK," Withers Worldwide, February 2, 2022, www. withersworldwide.com/en-gb/insight/read/comparing-foundation-minimum-distribution-in-the-us-canada-and-the-uk, accessed November 4, 2025.

59 Our World in Data, "Share of Population Living in Extreme Poverty," accessed February 20, 2023, ourworldindata.org/grapher/share-of-population-in-extreme-poverty.

60 Citi Global Perspectives and Solutions, "Philanthropy and the Global Economy: Opportunities in a World of Transition," Citi IGC, November 17, 2021, www.privatebank.citibank.com/newcpb-media/media/documents/insights/Philanthropy-and-global-economy.pdf, accessed November 4, 2025.

61 Max Roser et al., "Economic Growth," Our World in Data, 2015, accessed February 20, 2023, ourworldindata.org/economic-growth.

62 Max Roser and Esteban Ortiz-Ospina, "Income Inequality," Our World in Data, last modified October 2016, accessed February 20, 2023, ourworldindata.org/income-inequality.

63 Sjir Hoeijmakers, "The Case for Investing to Give Later," Effective Altruism Forum, July 20, 2020, forum.effectivealtruism.org/posts/CfLoq8nJBzRARohtQ, accessed November 4, 2025.

64 One might protest that these benefits should already be captured in our marginal cost-effectiveness curve. Very few cost-effectiveness analyses today capture the full range of benefits to the beneficiary, for example because they use DALYs (disability-adjusted life years) and focus only on health rather than income or happiness. Few capture benefits to others,

such as family members, communities, or animals. Few capture long-term benefits over decades or generations.

65 Senterra Funders, accessed November 4, 2025, www.senterrafunders.org.

66 Big Bang Philanthropy, accessed November 4, 2025, www.bigbangphilanthropy.org.

67 Agency Fund, accessed November 4, 2025, www.agency.fund/join-us.

68 Charity Entrepreneurship Seed Network, accessed November 4, 2025, www.seednetworkfunders.com.

69 Charity Entrepreneurship, accessed November 4, 2025, www.charityentrepreneurship.com/

70 AIM Mental Health Funding Circle, accessed November 4, 2025, www.mentalhealthfunders.com.

71 Strategic Animal Funding Circle, accessed November 4, 2025, www.animalfundingcircle.com.

72 EA Funds, "Scope and Limitations of EA Funds," Effective Altruism, accessed February 20, 2023, funds.effectivealtruism.org/scope-and-limitations.

73 Mulago Foundation, "How We Fund," www.mulagofoundation.org/how-we-fund, accessed November 4, 2025.

74 Justin Sandefur, "The Final Word on Microcredit?," Center for Global Development, January 22, 2015, www.cgdev.org/blog/final-word-microcredit, accessed November 4, 2025.